# SWINGIN' LONDON

# LONDON

## A Field Guide

# SWINGIN' LONDON
## A Field Guide

MARK WORDEN
&
ALFREDO MARZIANO

AMBERLEY

*In loving memory of Alastair and Mary Worden, who did many wonderful things, including taking their two youngest children to Kids in Gear during the Summer of Love.*

First published 2021

Amberley Publishing
The Hill, Stroud
Gloucestershire, GL5 4EP

www.amberley-books.com

British Library Cataloguing in Publication Data.
A catalogue record for this book is available from the British Library.

ISBN 978 1 3981 0683 3 (print)
ISBN 978 1 3981 0684 0 (ebook)

Typeset in 9pt on 12pt Sabon.
Typesetting and Origination by Amberley Publishing.
Printed in the UK.

# Introduction
# and Acknowledgements

This book endeavours to offer a practical guide to the locations (such as clubs, pubs, shops, restaurants, bars, offices, recording studios, performance venues, houses, etc.) that played a prominent role during the 'Swinging London' era of the 1960s. They have been divided up according to postcode. The research was based on a number of books (which are listed in the Bibliography at the end) and articles, but also on interviews with people who frequented the places in question. Sadly, some of the interviewees are no longer with us.

In addition to thanking all the people quoted in this book, not to mention the staff at various establishments and innocent bystanders on the street, the authors would also like to thank Derek Allen, Jamie Ambler, Riccardo Bertoncelli, Luca Biondi and other members of the Italian Floyd gang, Tom Bolton, Pier Andrea Canei, Ray Coggin, Sarah Coombes, Rosaria D'Amico, Richard Davenport-Hines, Mark Dezzani, Anthony Gardner, Claudio Giorgi, John Glover, Mary Hegarty, the late (and much missed) Leonie Jameson, Luigi Licci, Charles Liebling, Geoff Marshall, Mark Mason, Narinder Minhas, Joanna Moncrieff, Andrea Parente, Mike Patterson, Luigi Pedrazzi, Nicola and Simone Pittaluga, Daniel Richards, Carolina Samper, Carl Schonbeck, Hamish and Sally Scutt, Mike Taylor and the 'Amici Aperitivi', Adrian Wallwork, Paul Wells, Ben, Blair, Robert, Tim and Tommy Worden, and Franco Zanetti.

# W1: Fitzrovia

## The Post Office Tower
## No. 60 Cleveland Street
## London, W1T 4JZ

According to a plaque, 'The Post Office Tower was opened by the Right Honourable Harold Wilson OBE MP Prime Minister on the 8th October 1965.' It would subsequently become a symbol of both modern London and modern Britain. It also represented what Wilson would later call 'the white heat of the technological revolution,' even if construction work on the tower had begun in 1961, when a Conservative, Harold Macmillan, was still prime minister.

The top floor of the Post Office Tower was home to a revolving restaurant that was operated by Butlins. That could explain the quality of the food, as *Private Eye*'s Barry Fantoni explains:

> You'd book your table at 9 o'clock and you sat down to your chicken in a basket, or a glass of Cyprus sherry or red ruby wine from the Coop, and then you would sit there looking at Neasden, and then this amazing restaurant would turn round and, by the time you got your Black Forest gateau and Kenco coffee at the end of it, you'd be facing Stepney.

In addition to his work as a cartoonist and writer for *Private Eye*, Barry Fantoni also presented the TV show *A Whole Scene Going*, which would lead him to win an award from the now defunct music publication *Melody Maker* for TV Personality of the Year in September 1966. *Melody Maker* hosted the ceremony at the Post Office Tower restaurant. Paul McCartney also turned up to collect the award for Pop Group of the Year on behalf of the Beatles. But, as Barry Fantoni recalls,

> Something went wrong and by the time they came to the speeches, the man giving the speeches was facing Neasden and the people who were receiving them were facing Stepney. And for some reason they'd piled up all the chairs that weren't being used in the middle and so there was this assault course as people had to climb over the chairs to get their *Melody Maker* awards!

Undeterred, Paul McCartney returned to the restaurant on Monday 3 February 1969. On that occasion the Beatles' Apple label hosted a party for his discovery, Mary Hopkin. Hopkin had a big hit the previous year with the song 'Those Were the Days', and the party was for her debut album *Postcard*. Donovan, who wrote three of its tracks, attended, as did Jimi Hendrix. Hopkin later told *The Daily Telegraph*:

My family came down from Wales and in the throng of people we lost my 80-year-old grandmother, Blodwyn. When the crowd parted we saw her in the corner talking to Jimi Hendrix. Afterwards she said she had been talking to 'a nice little boy' who had been asking about milking the cows and feeding the chickens. I think he was fascinated by this funny little Welsh lady.

The Post Office Tower was also a popular film and television location. *Doctor Who* was the first to get in on the act. 'The War Machines', a four-part serial that was broadcast in June and July 1966, begins with the TARDIS time machine landing in Fitzroy Square and the First Doctor (played by William Hartnell) noticing with satisfaction that work on the tower has been completed since his last visit to London.

The Post Office Tower also appears in two films that were released in December 1967, namely *Bedazzled* and *A Smashing Time*. In *Bedazzled* Nicholas Spigott, who is in fact the Devil (played by Peter Cook), takes his victim, Stan Moon (Dudley Moore), to the top of the tower as it offers a vantage point for surveying the Home Counties and planning further mischief.

The tower's revolving restaurant provided the setting for the chaotic finale in *A Smashing Time*, for which George Melly wrote the screenplay. The film is a curious mix of pie-throwing slapstick comedy and a biting satire on the Swinging London scene. Yvonne (played by Lynn Redgrave) and Brenda (played by Melly's fellow Liverpudlian, Rita Tushingham) are two northern girls who head to the capital in search of fame and fortune. They eventually achieve their goal, despite some mishaps along the way. The characters they encounter include a Cockney fashion photographer, Tom Wabe (played by Michael York), who combines David Bailey with David Hemmings's imitation in *Blow-Up*, and an aristocratic boutique owner, Charlotte Brillig (played by Anna Quale), who is presumably based on Jane Ormsby-Gore, the daughter of Lord Harlech and the wife of Hung On You owner, Michael Rainey. Towards the end of their adventure a party is held for Yvonne at the restaurant but the two girls, who have grown to hate London, sneak into the control room and turn the revolving restaurant up to full speed. The groovy guests first feel nausea and are then thrown against the circular wall by the centrifugal force, while the prank causes a massive power cut throughout London (an idea enforced by a brief shot of Battersea Power Station). Yvonne and Brenda leave the tower and, as they walk along Charlotte Street at dawn, with the tower in the background, decide to use their return (train) tickets to go home to Bradford.

The Post Office Tower.

# The UFO Club
# No. 31 Tottenham Court Road
# London, W1T 1BX

The UFO Club first opened on Saturday 23 December 1966 (the line-up included Pink Floyd, who would become the club's first house band) and closed on Saturday 29 September 1967 (with, among others, Jeff Beck and Ten Years After). The club was the brainchild of two people: record producer and artist manager Joe Boyd and John 'Hoppy' Hopkins, who was also a co-founder of the underground paper *The International Times*. As Boyd explains:

> We decided to look for a place to open a club that would, once a week, have the kind of atmosphere that there was at the *International Times* [launch] party. And we went around, driving around, looking for the right place and we finally found this Irish dance hall in Tottenham Court Road called the Blarney Club. And it was down in the basement, and a very low ceiling, kind of gloomy room, but it had quite a big dance floor, a very small stage, and then it had a kind of hallway leading to a bar where you could sell soft drinks, things like that. And, from the beginning, we put on groups like Pink Floyd, we put on avant-garde jazz, oriental music, we showed films like W.C. Fields, Kurosawa films, we had improvisational groups, kind of conceptual happenings, all kinds of different things. And it was like the *International Times* party, only more so, because now a lot more ordinary people who, you know, wouldn't get invited to a thing like a party, just turned up and bought tickets. Everybody was so excited to see that there were people like them. Nobody realised there were so many freaks. There were light shows, and the kind of clichés of what we think of as '67, was really forming at that time and they were all manifested at UFO, and the first few months was a fantastic atmosphere, everybody was so happy and excited to find that, in a way, they had so many friends!

In 1967 Roger Bunn, who would later be the first bass guitarist in the group Roxy Music, was a member of Giant Sun Trolley, a jazz trio that frequently played at the UFO. Bunn died in 2005, but during a 2004 visit to the UFO site he recalled:

> We used to arrive at about 9 o'clock in the evening, watch the Floyd, a couple of other bands and then about 4 o'clock we would play three-piece avant-garde jazz, which would start off with one soft, long note on the double bass and continue for a couple of hours, sometimes, until about 6 o'clock in the morning, and we'd stroll out of here, throw our instruments into a car and head back to a somewhat acid-filled environment of Ladbroke Grove and Portobello Road.

Not surprisingly, the powers that be weren't particularly fond of the UFO Club. The summer of 1967 was also when the police, often in league with the *News of the World* newspaper, 'went for' the underground scene. 'Hoppy' went to prison, while the arrest of Mick Jagger prompted *The Times* to quote Alexander Pope in asking 'who breaks a butterfly on a wheel?'. That editorial (written by William Rees-Mogg) was published on 1 July – the same month the *News of the World* would print a blurred photo of a topless girl dancing at the UFO. At this point the police put pressure on the Blarney Club's manager, Irishman Joe Gannon, to stop renting his dance hall out to the UFO crowd and Gannon was obliged to follow their advice. After this UFO nights were held at the Roundhouse, which had hosted the original *International Times* party, but this experiment was also short-lived.

The UFO Club.

L'Etoile.

## L'Etoile

## No. 30 Charlotte Street

## London, W1T 2NG

This restaurant was classified as an 'In spot' in Piri Halasz's seminal Swinging London article in *Time* magazine in 1966. The following year she added (in her book *A Swinger's Guide to London*) that its two-star classic French cuisine could be enjoyed in the company of a friendly French-style cat that liked to rub against the legs of customers. *The London Spy* (1966), on the other hand, listed L'Etoile as one of London's pricier restaurants at £4 a head (including wine and a tip), but considered it 'value for money'. It also explained that London's French restaurants tended to be run by Italians, its Italian restaurants by Greeks and its Greek restaurants by Cypriots.

## The White Tower

## No. 1 Percy Street

## London, W1T 1DB

This Greek restaurant is included (along with Mirabelle and L'Etoile) in the list of 'other In spots' (after Trattoria Terrazza and Tiberio's) in Piri Halasz's 1966 *Time* article. She did, however, alter

The White Tower.

her view in *A Swinger's Guide to London* the following year. By then it had become 'crowded' and 'noisy' on account of her fellow Americans and so 'swingers' tended to avoid it during the tourist season. Len Deighton's *London Dossier* (1967) was more favourable, describing the food as impeccable and promising readers that there was a fair chance that they would run into the likes of Charlie Chaplin, Ingrid Bergman or Alfred Hitchcock. It also observed that 'patrons wearing polo neck sweaters and jeans' were 'not exactly encouraged'.

## Twiggy Enterprises
## Nos 22–23 Little Portland Street
## London, W1W 8BU

The story of the model Twiggy 'The Face of '66' is told in the entry on The House of Leonard Salon (see page 30). Twiggy's success was so rapid that that the same year she and her boyfriend and business partner Justin de Villeneuve opened a 'Twiggy' shop in Little Portland Street. It was also the headquarters of Twiggy Enterprises. Photos taken outside the shop in July 1967 show Twiggy posing with her Swedish double, Kerstin Lindberg. Kerstin was a sixteen-year-old schoolgirl who had won a Twiggy lookalike competition run by a Swedish paper. The prize included a trip to London and the chance to meet Twiggy, who was herself was only a year older.

Twiggy Enterprises.

# W1: Soho

## The Bag O'Nails
## No. 9 Kingly Street
## London, W1B 5PN

A plaque outside this club tells us that 'The Jimi Hendrix Experience first played here on 25th November, 1966,' while another says that 'Paul McCartney met Linda Eastman here on 15th May, 1967'. McCartney confirms this in *The Beatles Anthology*, adding that he used to like going there so that he could hang out with 'mates' like Pete Townsend, Zoot Money and Georgie Fame. Indeed, Georgie Fame and the Blue Fames were performing the night he met Linda. Paul also reveals that his romance with Linda began when he asked her to join him and a group of friends who were going on to the Speakeasy.

Steampacket and Holy Trinity organist Brian Auger remembers that the Bag O'Nails was 'an interesting place. I think it was the Gunnell Brothers, who ran the Flamingo, who ran the Bag O'Nails, so we kind of rotated in these places,' while for Deviants lead singer Mick Farren, there was a whiff of gangland in the air. It was 'a bit Ronnie and Reggie [Kray], but then again Chas

The Bag O'Nails.

Chadler knew Ronnie and Reggie. Actually, it was where Hendrix did his first show. So we were kind of tolerated there'.

Fantoni and Dallas's *Swinging London: A Guide to Where the Action Is* (1967) tells us that its hours of business were 10.30 p.m. to 4 a.m., although alcohol could no longer be served after 3 a.m. Spirits were 3s 6d; wine was 30s a bottle. Membership was 3 guineas; admission was 10s for members, £1 for guests.

## Trattoria Terrazza
## No. 19 Romilly Street
## London, W1D 5AE

According to Alasdair Scott Sutherland, author of the book *The Spaghetti Tree: Mario and Franco and the Trattoria Revolution*, this establishment played a pivotal role in the restaurant history of both London and the UK. He argues that prior to the opening of the country's first informal Italian 'trattoria' dining out had been a drab, formal affair.

The 'Tratt' opened in 1959. Its founders, Mario Cassandro and Franco Lagattolla, had previously worked (as sommelier and maitre d' respectively) at the Mirabelle in Curzon Street. They were joined by another Mirabelle veteran, Alvaro Maccioni. Len Deighton mentioned the restaurant in his 1961 spy thriller *The Ipcress File* and its fame grew exponentially over the course of the decade. Piri Halasz's 1966 Swinging London article for *Time* magazine placed it at the top of a list of 'unpretentious but ever so in' little restaurants in Soho, mentioning its Positano Room, which was located in the basement. In her 1967 book, she said it had been the 'In-est place in town' the previous summer and that, if you were lucky, you might bump into Ursula Andress, Dudley Moore and James Mason.

Not surprisingly, 'the Tratt' features in other contemporary guidebooks. Dallas and Fantoni (1967) tell us that it's the best place for seeing models, film stars and publicists, while *Len Deighton's London Dossier* (1967) calls it 'friendly, bustling and even exciting,' as well as 'not too expensive' and *The New London Spy* (1966) lists it among the restaurants where '£2 should cover you'.

Trattoria Terrazza.

## Thea Porter
## No. 8 Greek Street
## London, W1D 4DG

> Thea Porter herself was a really charming lady who went out east and came back with beautiful furniture, beautiful fabrics, and made them up into beautiful clothes; expensive, too. So all the silk would feature hand-sewn patterns. It wasn't like a real cheapo kaftan from the antique market or something like that. These were real ones. They were really expensive.

That is how Jenny Fabian remembers Thea Porter, who ran a small but fashionable boutique in Greek Street. Fabian also mentions the shop in her cult novel *Groupie* (1969), saying that it 'specialises in beautiful materials from the East'. Today she recalls: 'It wasn't exactly a meeting place, but if you went in there to look and buy something you nearly always bumped into somebody like Roger Daltrey, or one of the Pink Floyd; they had a lot of their clothes made there. So it was a very important place. It was a cut above your Granny Takes a Trip, or your Quorum. It was the designer label of the underground clothes, as you would call it now.'

Nor did the diminutive Thea Porter cater to just rock aristocracy. According to an article by Marian Christy in *The Ledger* in 1975, her clientele included Princess Margaret (who never actually visited the store) and Elizabeth Taylor (who did). Both loved her kaftans and she is generally credited with making the Middle Eastern look fashionable.

It is believed that Porter's love of that look came from her unconventional upbringing. She was born Dorothea Naomi Seale in Jerusalem in 1927 to French and English missionary parents, and grew up in Damascus. She went to London to study for a degree, but returned to the Middle East after marrying a diplomat, Robert Porter. That ended in divorce and she came back to London in the 1960s with her young daughter.

The Greek Street boutique was only one of the ventures in a varied but commercially unsuccessful career. She opened a store in New York in the 1970s. That failed, as did Thea Porter Decorations, a later business venture in London. She was diagnosed with Alzheimer's in 1994 and died in a nursing home in 2000.

Thea Porter.

# The Establishment Club
# No. 18 Greek Street,
# London, W1D 4DS

As a City of Westminster Heritage Foundation plaque reminds us, No. 18 Greek Street was the site of the Establishment Club from 1961 to 1964. The club was co-founded by Nicholas Luard and the leading satirist of the day, Peter Cook.

The Establishment Club opened for business in October 1961 – the same month that Cook and Luard helped launch *Private Eye*. Staff writer and cartoonist Barry Fantoni recalls: 'We were at 22 Greek Street and the Establishment was next door and we had all these people coming over like Lenny Bruce, and Dudley (Moore) would play there in the evenings. And it was quite a hot little scene, that whole area was strip clubs and prostitutes were still on the streets.'

In actual fact No. 18 Greek Street was a strip club prior to the Establishment Club's arrival. The notorious Kray twins paid Cook a visit but, as he later told Clive James, he thanked them for their kind offer of protection, and 'never saw them again.' Perhaps the Krays were in awe of Cook and Luard's public school and Cambridge backgrounds. Certainly Barry Fantoni, another home-grown Londoner, thought that the Establishment was frequented by toffs:

> Its clientele was just about everybody who wanted to be anybody, like full of wannabes, as you would expect, and a lot of upper-class people who could afford the prices because it was really an upper-class place, it was really for debutantes and yahoos, I suppose, and you heard that kind of barky, squeaky voice of the upper classes. Very few working-class people went up there, they weren't interested, they'd got their pubs and their own gig, and they weren't interested in American comedians. Actors went there, people after hours went there, performers who'd been working in the West End. I didn't actually like it very much.

No. 18 Greek Street did serve, very briefly, as the office of *Private Eye*, but the building was also the location of the studio where Lewis Morley took the famous photo of 'Profumo girl' Christine Keeler, in which her nudity is covered by the Arne Jacobsen chair upon which she sits. According to Lewis Morley (in a statement for the V&A, which accorded his photo 'iconic' status), the studio

The Establishment Club.

was on the first floor, the Establishment Club on the ground floor, while the Dudley Moore Trio and other musical acts played in the basement.

Musician Brian Auger, who often played there, recalls: 'There were three jazz trios that would rotate, you know, and when we weren't playing downstairs or at one of the places, we would go upstairs in the theatre and we would sit down and Peter Cook and Dudley Moore would be at the table and they'd have these insane conversations and we would sit there just absolutely falling about, man, it was crazy!'

## *Private Eye*
## No. 22 Greek Street
## London, W1D 4DZ

During the '60s *Private Eye*'s offices were at No. 22 Greek Street, in the heart of Soho. Barry Fantoni, who created such classics as the appalling poetry of E. J. Thribb (who, he says, was based on 'people like Seamus Heaney and Ted Hughes') and Neasden F. C. (which was inspired by his 'life-long love of Millwall'), joined the magazine in 1963. When asked why the *Private Eye* staff had chosen Greek Street, in an area best known for its strip clubs, he said:

> The first office, I think, was the bedroom of Willie Rushton's flat (at 28 Scarsdale Villas, Kensington – ed.). And I think there was a short period they had a room somewhere. Cheap, I mean, Soho was so cheap. I lived for a while in Monmouth Street, which was just round the corner, and it was a shared toilet and shared kitchen, and I think it was five shillings a week for the bedroom. And I don't think they paid more than about 10 quid a week for these rooms,

Private Eye.

which were over a strip club at 22 Greek Street. And the jokes were punctuated by this man who continually shouted, throughout the day, '14 lovely girls, all naked, all the same!' And I could never understand why he said, 'All the same!' As if it that would be a draw, you know, I would have thought, 'All different!' But he actually shouted out, 'All the same!' I mean, Christopher Booker got mad once, and, before he got fired, he threw a typewriter out the window and it very narrowly missed this man on the head! It could have all changed dramatically, had he scored a direct hit!

*Private Eye* left No. 22 Greek Street and moved to No. 6 Carlisle Street in 1984.

# Happening 44
# No. 44 Gerrard Street
# London, W1D 5QD

In the words of Mick Farren: 'There was a small club which we used to play at called Happening 44 on Gerrard Street, right by the old Ronnie Scott Club, and that was an ex-strip club.'

Farren offered a more detailed account in his memoir *Give the Anarchist a Cigarette*, in which he described the 'weirdest hippy dungeon ever', where flower children briefly rubbed shoulders with more traditional Soho residents like call girls and 'serious gangsters' from the Richardson family.

Happening 44 was run by Jack Braceland, who headed a company called Fiveacre Lights. This was named after the Fiveacre Woods nudist colony that Braceland and his wife operated near Watford.

Farren's group the Deviants had the Saturday night residency at Happening 44. They performed there, for example, on Saturday 3 June, 1967, in a show that was advertised in the *International Times* the previous day, with an invitation to 'Tune in, Drop in, Come to Life, Love, Be-in with The Colour of Sound, The Sounds of Colour, Rave Groups, Exotic Entertainment, Movies, Strobe, Discs, Groovy Food, Fantastic Decorations, The Astounding Slides of Ron Henderson and the Fiveacre Light Show.'

The Soft Machine and Fairport Convention also played at Happening 44, but the club was only open for a few months.

Happening 44.

The Flamingo Club.

## The Flamingo Club
## No. 33 Wardour Street
## London, W1D 6PU

A City of Westminster Heritage Foundation plaque at No. 33 Wardour tells us: 'This building was the location of The Flamingo Club (1957–1967) The home of Jazz and Rhythm & Blues. Founded by Jeffrey S. Kruger MBE, a pioneer of the British Music Industry.'

The club had originally opened in the basement of the Mapleton Hotel in nearby Coventry Street in 1952, but when it moved to Wardour Street it was to see plenty of action. In the early 1960s it was managed by Rik Gunnell, who would later run the Bag O'Nails. According to *The Beatles' London*, the ground floor and basement were dedicated to jazz, while the upstairs was given over to the All Nighter Club where Georgie Fame and the Blues Flames (who were also managed by Gunnell) played on a regular basis. Its clientele included a large number of West Indians and black American GIs.

This is evident in the comments of contemporary guidebooks. *The New London Spy* (1966) argues that 'the West Indian half of the clientele keep the jazz music standards high,' while according to Jane Wilson's chapter 'Teenagers' in *Len Deighton's London Dossier*, 'the negroes' (this word was still considered acceptable in 1967) had moved there from the Marquee and it was the 'home of Georgie Fame and the Blue Flames, and Zoot Money and the Big Roll Band'. Piri Halasz's *A Swinger's Guide to London* tells us that 'next door is a discotheque, the Whiskey-à-Go-go which has long been known as place where au pairs come to meet English boys, usually pseudostudents or lonely West Indians'. She wrote these comments in 1967 – the year that the club closed.

## Carnaby Street
## London, W1F

A green City of Westminster plaque at the south end of Carnaby Street reads: 'John Stephen 1934–2004. Founder of Carnaby Street as world centre for men's fashion in the 1960s.' This is no idle boast as John Stephen really did put this previously unremarkable street on the map, even if this came about largely by accident.

According to another City of Westminster plaque on the wall of No. 5 Newburgh Street, it all began there: 'Vince's Man Shop: Bill Green opened his first menswear boutique here in 1954. As one of the earliest male fashion shops in London, it started the Swinging 60s fashion revolution in Carnaby Street.' The shop, which mainly sold swimming trunks, was popular with Soho's gay community, who liked to gather at the nearby Marshall Street baths. For its advertising campaign, Vince's used a muscular model from Edinburgh by the name of Sean Connery. A young Glaswegian, John Stephen, joined the staff and a couple of years later opened his own place with his partner in business and life, Bill Franks. This was in Beak Street, but when the shop burnt down in a fire in 1957 they moved round the corner to No. 5 Carnaby Street.

They were to expand and open several shops. According to George Melly (writing in December 1969, in his book *Revolt into Style*), things really took off in 1963 when Carnaby Street became popular with the Mods. The trend was originally for men's clothing, with women's clothes shops coming later. The street was, however, to lose its lustre within a few years. Melly wrote, 'The 'in' group wouldn't have been seen dead in Carnaby Street by 1966.' Perhaps that had something to do with the Kinks song 'Dedicated Follower of Fashion', which was released on Friday 25 February. The lyrics included the comment, 'Everywhere the Carnabetian Army marches on, each one a dedicated follower of fashion.'

Nevertheless, Carnaby Street was still sufficiently in for its shops to appear in assorted guidebooks in 1967. David Johnson and Roger Dunkley's *Gear Guide 1967*, for example, was a 'Hip-pocket Guide to Britain's Swinging Fashion Scene' and it naturally concentrated on Carnaby Street and the King's Road. *Gear Guide* lists nineteen Carnaby Street establishments and a further eight in the surrounding area, including Vince's, which was still going strong in Newburgh Street. *Gear Guide* is not to be confused with a shop called Gear at No. 35 Carnaby Street, which Dallas and Fantoni listed in their section on 'female fashion', although it also did 'Pine furniture £5 to £65, Brass beds £45, kitchen paraphernalia, children's clothing'. The children's section was known as 'Kids in Gear'. Lord John (which in fact had nothing to do with John Stephens) at No. 43 was also popular. This too has a green City of Westminster plaque: 'During the Swinging 60s fashion revolution this building housed the Gold Brothers' iconic store, famous for its trend-setting mod clothes and its psychedelic mural.' The said piece was by Om Tentacle, who were also responsible for the artwork at Flying Dragon on the King's Road. Topper, a shoe store at No. 45 run by the very young Steve Topper, was another favourite. Its clients included French star Johnny Halliday, the Small Faces and Jimmy Tarbuck (who had been in the same class as John Lennon at primary school in Liverpool).

John Stephen's main store at No. 52/55 likewise got plenty of coverage in the guidebooks, even though it had several branches, including one on the King's Road.

Vince's Man Shop, Newburgh Street.

Gear, Carnaby Street.

Lord John, Carnaby Street.

Topper, Carnaby Street.

John Stephens, Carnaby Street.

## The Marquee Club
## No. 90 Wardour Street
## London, W1F 0TH

The Marquee Club moved from No. 165 Oxford Street (where the Stones played their first live gig, on Friday 12 July 1962) to No. 90 Wardour Street in the spring of 1964. According to George Melly's book *Revolt into Style* it was here that 'British R and B established itself at a time when, in the wider field of pop, the Beatles were carrying all before them.' For Jane Wilson, on the other hand (in the 'Teenagers' chapter in *Len Deighton's London Dossier*, 1967), this venue, with its 'murky' entrance and 'hot, damp and salty' air, was 'the tabernacle and heart of London's blood-music.'

The bill for the first night on Friday 13 March featured blues legend Sonny Boy Williamson, the Yardbirds, and Long John Baldry and his Hoochie Coochie Men (the group, which numbered Rod Stewart among its members, would later evolve into Steampacket), who had previously played at No. 165 Oxford Street. Subsequent performers at No. 90 Wardour Street included The Who, the Spencer Davis Group, Pink Floyd (first as the Abdabs in 1964 and later as part of a 'Spontaneous Underground' event in March 1966), the Moody Blues, King Crimson, the Jimi Hendrix Experience and Led Zeppelin.

According to Dallas and Fantoni (1967) you could enjoy this great music for an admission fee of between 5 and 10 shillings, while a six-month membership cost 5s.

The Marquee Club.

# W1: Mayfair

## Sybilla's
## No. 9 Swallow Street
## London, W1B 4DE

This was arguably the most exclusive nightclub of the lot. Its partners included Beatle George Harrison (who was given a small stake), aristocratic jockey Sir William Piggott-Brown and disc jockey Alan 'Fluff' Freeman. It was named in honour of Sybilla Edmonstone, the heiress to the Marshall Field department store empire in Chicago.

The investors were found by Kevin MacDonald Associates, a triumvirate consisting of two young advertising types, the aforementioned Kevin McDonald and Terence Howard, and property dealer Bruce Higham. It took them a while to find backers, but the club finally opened with a private party on Wednesday 22 June 1966. The guest list included the Beatles, the Stones, Julie Christie, Michael Caine, Mary Quant and her husband Alexander Plunkett-Greene, Cathy McGowan, David Bailey and Terence Donovan, Leslie Caron, Tara and Nicky Browne, Michael Rainey and Jane Ormsby-Gore, Roman Polanski and the young gossip columnist Nigel Dempster. That year *The New London Spy* observed that 'all the stars of London's discothequocracy, aristocracy and plutocracy constellate there' and commented on its 'much-heralded décor' by David Milinaric.

In spite of this glorious start, Kevin MacDonald committed suicide on Saturday 15 October (although it has been claimed that he was murdered). And yet the club was still looking good in 1967. *A Swinger's Guide to London* describes it as a 'blue-lit basement aquarium' with strip lights that point upwards from the floor, thereby offering spectators an excellent view of the miniskirts on display.

Sybilla's.

We also learn that Vanessa Redgrave was a member. Fantoni and Dallas tell us that membership cost 7 guineas. There was a cover charge of £1 and meals, including wine, cost approximately 30s.

But Sybilla's success was relatively short-lived and it closed in August 1968. Various other clubs have occupied the premises since then.

## No. 3 Savile Row

## London, W1S 3PB

The Beatles gave their last live performance on the roof of this building on Thursday 30 January 1969. This was because, as of 18 July the previous year, it had been the headquarters of their Apple Corps organisation. Prior to that the company had been based at No. 95 Wigmore Street.

No. 3 Savile Row was a combination of rehearsal space and business office. It was, for example, the home of Apple Records, which recorded the likes of James Taylor, Mary Hopkin, Badfinger and Billy Preston (who was part of the rooftop line-up). Yet Apple Corps tends to be remembered more for its disastrous experiment in 'western communism'. The Beatles had been advised to invest in other people's ideas as a tax write-off. As a result, numerous young entrepreneurs turned up and presented madcap schemes. Apple Corps's open-door policy encouraged a young American called Don DiLello to show up one day and ask for a job. He was immediately appointed 'house hippy'. He decided to keep a diary and later shared its contents in *The Longest Cocktail Party: An Insider's Diary of The Beatles, Their Million-dollar Apple Empire and its Wild Rise and Fall...* which Noel Gallagher described, not unreasonably, as 'a fucking brilliant book'. It chronicles such surreal events as an unexpected visit from a Californian chapter of the Hells' Angels, another from film star Lauren Bacall, and the adventures of a young hippy family who camped out in the waiting room for weeks.

Apple Corps, like the Beatles, began to disintegrate. Tough New York exec Allen Klein was brought in to steady a sinking ship, but this created further tensions with the group. The Beatles split in 1970 and Apple Corps left the building in 1972.

No. 3 Savile Row later became a branch of Abercrombie. There is even a display of Beatles memorabilia at the entrance. You can visit all the floors of the building, except the famous roof.

No. 3 Savile Row.

No. 23 Mount Street.

## No. 23 Mount Street
## London W1K 2HE

'We used to go to Robert Fraser's lovely flat in Mount Street, and meet Kenneth Anger there. I first met Paul McCartney there.' That was how Nigel Lesmoir-Gordon, a young resident of No. 101 Cromwell Road, recalled No. 23 Mount Street. For Keith Richard (writing in his autobiography *Life*), it was 'the salon of the period,' while for American writer Terry Southern, quoted in Harriet Vyner's biography, *Groovy Bob: The Life and Times of Robert Fraser*, it was 'a veritable mecca for the movers and groovers of the sixties scene'. In addition to Messrs. Anger, Southern, McCartney, Richards and Miss Anita Pallenberg, the movers and groovers included William Burroughs, Allen Ginsberg, David Hockney and Dennis Hopper.

Keith Richards also describes the flat's collection of 'fantastic objects,' and Fraser's impressive wardrobe of double-breasted suits, which often contained 'spare jacks'. A jack, he explains, is a sixth of a gram of heroin.

## Mr Fish
## No. 17 Clifford Street
## London, W1S 3RQ

Mr Fish sold far-out but expensive men's clothing to the upper echelons of Swinging London society. The shop was run by Michael Fish, who had learnt his trade at nearby Turnbull & Asser, with the financial backing of Barry Sainsbury. Mr Fish opened for business in 1966 and catered to rock aristocrats like Mick Jagger (who wore an androgynous white Michael Fish smock when he and other members of the Rolling Stones performed at the Hyde Park free concert tribute in 1969, after the death of Brian Jones) and the Beatles, as well as to real aristocrats like Lord Snowdon and Patrick Lichfield. Snowdon and Lichfield's fellow photographer David Bailey was a client, as were the actors Terence Stamp and James Fox. The shop was particularly famous for its ruffled shirts and printed ties. According to Dallas and Fantoni (1967) the stock included 'shirts from 6 gns, ties from 2 gns, suits, jackets and overcoats ready to wear and bespoke'. Mr Fish seemed to have a winning formula. By 1969 the shop had an annual turnover of £250,000, but success was short-lived and it closed in the early 1970s.

Mr Fish.

## Annabel's
## No. 44 Berkeley Square
## London, W1J 5AR

Annabel's features in Piri Halasz' 1966 Swinging London article for *Time* magazine. In 'SCENE ONE' she describes it as 'London's leading discotheque,' even if she gives greater emphasis to the Clermont Club upstairs. *Len Deighton's London Dossier* (1967), on the other hand, calls it 'London's smartest discotheque,' while adding that it is too 'restrained' and 'expensive' to be 'the most popular'. In 1967 Halasz observed that the dinners are 'excellent'. She recommends the Steak Diane (which George Harrison is known to have enjoyed) washed down with the Chamberlin '59. Dinner in 1967 cost around £5. Annabel's was, Halasz wrote, 'not only fashionable, but genuinely first class'.

Annabel's first-class nature was doubtless due to its location (a Palladian town house in Berkeley Square designed by William Kent in 1742), as well as its ownership. It was opened in 1963 by Old Etonian Mark Birley, who named it after his wife, Annabel Vane-Tempest-Stewart, the sister of the Marquess of Londonderry. Birley's sister, Maxine, had married a Frenchman and become Maxine de la Falaise. She worked as a model in the 1950s and with Andy Warhol in the 1970s. Her daughter, Loulou de la Falaise, was also part of 'the scene'.

Annabel's was an exclusive, members-only club. The Beatles enjoyed going there because they were less likely to be bothered by fans, even if George was turned away on New Year's Eve in 1966 as he wasn't wearing a tie. According to *The Beatles' London*, he left, along with Patti, her suitor Eric Clapton and Brian Epstein, and went to the less exclusive Lyons Corner House in the West End. Other people who have passed through Annabel's hallowed doors include Frank Sinatra, Muhammad Ali, Prince Charles and Richard Nixon. When George Melly visited in 1965 he spotted Paul Getty and Lucien Freud.

Annabel's also gets a brief mention in Canadian author Mordecai Richler's 1968 Swinging London novel, *Cocksure*. One of the characters takes a taxi to 'the discotheque in Berkeley Square' but slips off without paying the fare.

Annabel's and the
Clermont Club.

# The Clermont Club

# No. 44 Berkeley Square

# London, W1J 5AR

'SCENE ONE' of Piri Halasz's 1966 *Time* magazine article describes a 'handsome son of a peer' who wins £210,00 at 'chemmy' (chemin de fer) at the Clermont Club. He decides to leave but, after climbing into his chauffeur-driven Bentley, he realises that he has forgotten his winnings chit. He heads back into the club, starts playing again and loses £450,000.

The Clermont Club had been opened in 1962 by John Aspinall, who had already made plenty of money from illegal card games for the lords and ladies of Mayfair in the 1950s. John Aspinall lobbied to have gambling legalised and was able to obtain a licence for a club after the subsequent Betting and Gaming Act of 1960. At the Clermont Club he continued to work with an aristocratic clientele whom he allegedly fleeced, with the help of gangsters, thanks to a marked card system known as 'The Big Edge'. Other Clermont clients who may have lost their money include Peter Sellers, Lord Boothby, Bond creator Ian Fleming (who died in 1964) and the artist Lucian Freud. Princess Margaret also visited, as did the Greek heiress Athina Livanos. She was the former of wife of Aristotle Onassis but in the 1960s she was married to the Marquess of Blandford, who later became the Duke of Marlborough.

# The Mirabelle Restaurant

# No. 56 Curzon Street

# London, W1Y 7PF

Legend has it that Brian Epstein dined at the Mirabelle not long after the Beatles had received their MBEs (on Tuesday October 26 1965). He wasn't honoured (possibly because he was Jewish and homosexual, but probably because he wasn't a Beatle) and an unnamed actor who'd had a lot to drink is alleged to have commented loudly: 'Look at that little boy over there – he couldn't get an MBE'.

The Mirabelle appeared in the most expensive category in the 'Eating Out in London' section of *The New London Spy* (1966). It was listed as one of the establishments where 'you will have a good meal expensively served and pay £4 a head including wine and tip'.

The Mirabelle.

In fact it had been serving expensive food since opening in 1936. Guests in previous decades had included Orson Welles and Winston Churchill. The restaurant's other claim to fame is that it was here that Trattoria La Terrazza's founders, Mario Cassandro and Franco Lagattolla first met. As Alasdair Scott Sutherland recounts in his book *The Spaghetti Tree*, they were colleagues before deciding to open their own place in 1959.

The Mirabelle formed part of the building occupied by the Curzon Plaza Hotel. It closed in 2008, officially 'for renovation', but was demolished in 2018.

# Tiberio

# No. 22 Queen Street

# London, W1J 5PP

'The Tiberio was the very, very upmarket restaurant that Mario and Franco opened in Queen Street, Mayfair, and it was like a palace. It was £3 for two at the Terrazza: it was £8 at the Tiberio. And it was full of kings and princes and royalty.'

So says Alasdair Scott Sutherland, author of the book, *The Spaghetti Tree: Mario and Franco and the Trattoria Revolution*, which gives Tiberio's opening date as 20 December 1962. He also explains that the Tiberio was an attempt to challenge the supremacy of another Mayfair restaurant, the French Mirabelle, where the two Italians had worked before opening 'The Tratt' in 1959.

As for the Tiberio's royal clientele, Scott Sutherland recalls:

There was dancing at the Tiberio. There was a small band that started playing at 11.30, like the old-fashioned dinner and dance, and they went on till 2 o' clock and that was when they closed. And one evening there was a special bongo player drummer or something who was being part of an act, and suddenly there's a woman who jumps up, and John Wayne is over there on the back, a woman jumps and starts dancing with her partner frenziedly to this exotic music that' s going 'Tikka-tikka-tikka-tikka-tikka' and Franco, who' s standing at the back, he realises who it is, and she doesn't realise that it's actually an entertainment you're supposed to watch and it isn't just music for dancing. And it's Princess Margaret, and she's out there, you know, with her 'Princess Margaret Set' having a fine old time.

He quietens down the music and it's very discreet and nobody feels embarrassed and Princess Margaret goes to sit down again. Then John Wayne is sitting there with his chin on his chest, he

Tiberio.

sits there, still talking about this, and it' s 2 o'clock, he doesn't want to go home at all, and he says to Mario, or Franco, he says, 'Would you have someone go round to the Connaught and fetch me my chess set and bring it round here?' And Franco says: 'It's a restaurant, Duke, you know, we have to close, the boys all have to go home!' So John Wayne pulls out a couple of £100 bills and leaves them for the boys and says: 'Fetch the chess set!'

# The Saddle Room
# No. 7 Hamilton Place
# London, W1J 7DR

The Saddle Room, which opened its doors in 1961, has been called London's first discotheque. It was set up by Helene Cordet, whom *The New London Spy* (1966) described as 'the Queen of Clubs,' and Major Peter Davies, 'a 'horse-riding enthusiast'. The book called the place 'sophisticated and inclined to be a bit debby'.

The Saddle Room was given a paragraph in Piri Halasz's *A Swinger's Guide to London* (1967). Halasz admired the fact that it had survived 'passing fads,' and that it was spacious, unlike other

The Saddle Room.

London clubs. She also noted that regular membership was 22s 6d, while the entrance fee and the first drink came to £1.

The Saddle Room closed in the early 1980s. The building has since been demolished. It is now the site of the Four Seasons Hotel.

## The Robert Fraser Gallery
## No. 69 Duke Street
## London, W1K 5NX

'SCENE FOUR' of Piri Halasz's 1966 Swinging London article for *Time* magazine took place at 'Robert Fraser's Gallery in Duke Street'. It describes 'Jane Ormsby-Gore, 23' who 'pops into a cocktail party' at the gallery. Fraser himself was interviewed for the piece, telling the world that London 'has something that New York used to have: everybody wants to be there'.

Fraser would achieve a different type of fame the following year. He was arrested (and subsequently given a six-month prison sentence for the possession of heroin) during the Redlands bust – a police raid on Keith Richards' Sussex home on Sunday 12 February 1967. The photo (taken in late June) of Fraser and Mick Jagger handcuffed together in the back of a police van en route from Lewes prison to Chichester Magistrates' Court would acquire iconic status. Richard Hamilton (one of many artists represented by Fraser) would use it for his 'Swingeing London' series of posters and paintings. The image provides the cover for Harriet Vyner's book *Groovy Bob: The Life and Times of Robert Fraser*. Vyner tells the story of Fraser's privileged background: Eton (even though his family was considered 'new money') and the army, his spectacularly promiscuous homosexuality and his rise in the art world. After leaving the army, Fraser worked for an art dealer in New York, but moved back to London where (with family money) he opened his own gallery (on premises previously occupied by a chemist). He soon established himself as an exciting avant-garde dealer at a time when the London art scene was still pretty stuffy. He introduced Britain to Andy Warhol and Jim Dine, but also promoted British artists like the aforementioned Hamilton, Bridget Riley and Peter Blake. Indeed, Fraser was the 'art director' of the *Sgt. Pepper* cover shoot, at the Chelsea Manor Studio (on Thursday March 30 1967) for which Blake, like many of Fraser's artists, didn't receive much money.

Nor did Fraser's Beatle connection end there. He liked to sell art to pop stars and introduced Paul McCartney to the work of René Magritte (which would provide the inspiration for the Apple logo). He also had a hand in Yoko Ono's 1966 exhibition at the Indica Gallery, where she met John Lennon.

The Robert Fraser Gallery.

And yet many artists actively disliked Fraser. Barry Fantoni, for example, recalls that 'Robert Fraser was a difficult man. I was glad when they sent him to prison, only on a very personal level. He promised me an exhibition and I painted 20 pictures for it, and then he reneged, he backed down, for reasons I never fully understood'.

The gallery went out of business in 1969, and Fraser spent a lot of time in India. He returned to London in the early 1980s and had a second stab at the art scene, but died of AIDS-related complications in 1986.

# The Embassy of the United States
# No. 24 Grosvenor Square
# London, W1A 2LQ

The 'Embassy of the United States to the Court of St. James's' was the scene of a number of anti-Vietnam War demonstrations in the 1960s. The first took place on Sunday 3 July 1966 and James Clough, who was then a student at the Chelsea School of Art, decided to go along. He recalls:

> I was with a group of about five or six friends and we were chanting, we were quite merry, really, but the big objective was to make our presence felt in Grosvenor Square, right in front of the American Embassy. The square must have been pretty full that afternoon. The cops were on their horses and there were police cordons. I don't know how it happened but I finished up at the front of the demonstration and was nabbed by some cops and arrested and bundled into a Black Maria with other protesters, of course, and we were taken down to some police station. I was terrified and we spent a few hours in this awful hot cell. I think there must have been about 20 or 30 of us.

A few days later James Clough was summoned to appear at Marylebone Magistrates' Court where, on the advice of his father, he pleaded guilty to the charge of assaulting a police officer, even though he hadn't assaulted anyone. This led to a one-month prison sentence, which he served at Wormwood Scrubs. After his release he spent a year in Canada, where he continued to be active in the anti-Vietnam War movement. He returned to London in 1967 and got involved in both the International Marxist Group and the Vietnam Solidarity Campaign: 'When I told them about my month in Wormwood Scrubs, they saw it as a big medal!' He worked at their offices at No. 49 Rivington Street and, when they decided to stage another march on the US Embassy (beginning in Trafalgar Square on Sunday 22 October 1967), he got to design the poster.

The US Embassy.

James Clough also went on that march, in addition to taking part in the 'Battle of Grosvenor Square' on Sunday 17 March 1968. By now political protests were erupting all over the world. A few weeks later Martin Luther King Jr would be assassinated in Memphis, while the student revolt would explode in Paris in May. The Vietnam War had escalated with the Tet offensive and this galvanised the anti-war movement.

As Deviants lead singer and *International Times* (*IT*) journalist Mick Farren recounted in his memoir, *Give the Anarchist a Cigarette*, the protesters gathered in Trafalgar Square to listen to speeches by Vanessa Redgrave and Tariq Ali. Farren admits that he and his fellow Deviant Sandy (Duncan Sanderson) skipped this bit, preferring to join the march at Centre Point, after it had made its way up the Charing Cross Road. It then turned left along Oxford Street and turned south into North Audley Street with a view to reaching Grosvenor Square. The police tried to block the 25,000 marchers and at this point battle commenced. Police horses charged the protesters, and by the end of the day eighty-six people had been injured and 200 arrests had been made. As on previous occasions the police seemed to enjoy the scrap, and they were not alone: later on, a relatively new social group, the skinheads, waved US flags and beat up any stray protesters they could lay their hands on (in something of a parallel with the pro-war, hippy-hating Hells Angels in the United States).

Many witnesses were shocked by what they saw. As (Barry) Miles, co-founder of the Indica Gallery and the *IT*, says: 'It's true, there's nothing more scary than a great gang of mounted police charging at you, but I think the Vietnam War was probably the last real big issue that the whole of the left was behind.'

For Pink Floyd drummer Nick Mason, on the other hand, the Grosvenor Square riots were more about the loss of innocence. He recalls:

> I had certainly my first experience of realising that the police could not be trusted and that lies would be told and that was to do with CND and protests of the period. I remember there being absolute denial that the police had charged a group of protesters in Grosvenor Square when they absolutely had. You know, anyone who was there heard the word 'Charge!' saw the horses coming forward and then watched the news that night as some, you know, bloody superior officer said, 'Oh, no, no, no, nothing like that!' I have to say that was a real eye-opener because I was brought up with the view that policemen were there to help you and tell you the time and make sure you got home OK!

And yet there was at least one moment of traditional police civility that day. In his 1970 book *The Pendulum Years: Britain and the Sixties*, *The Times* columnist Bernard Levin tells the story of a protester who tried to smoke. He placed the cigarette in his mouth but was unable to reach for the matches in his pocket as he was being crushed by the crowd around him. Not only that, he found that his particular section of the crowd was being pushed towards the line of policemen. Somewhat to his surprise, an officer patrolling behind the line took out a lighter, reached over his comrades and lit the demonstrator's cigarette, with the words 'Allow me'.

# The House of Leonard Salon
# No. 6 Upper Grosvenor Street
# London, W1K 2LJ

In the 1960s this Georgian terrace house was occupied by Raphael and Leonard (also known as the House of Leonard and Leonard of Mayfair), a hair salon that helped create one of Swinging London's most iconic figures.

The story is the stuff of legend. The salon was run by Leonard Lewis, who had previously worked for Vidal Sassoon at No. 171 New Bond Street. There a fellow colleague, Nigel Davies, had been

The House of Leonard.

fired, prior to changing his name to the more glamorous Justin de Villeneuve. At some stage in 1965 de Villeneuve met a sixteen-year-old schoolgirl from Neasden called Lesley Hornby who had a Saturday job in a Queensway hair salon. He thought she had an amazingly beautiful face and tried to set her up as a model – unsuccessfully at first. He therefore decided that she should change both her hairstyle and her name. He chose Twiggy, on account of the fact that she was very skinny.

De Villeneuve booked her at the very posh Leonard of Mayfair, which, he discovered, was run by his old friend from Vidal Sasoon days, Leonard Lewis. The styling session took place in January 1966. Leonard liked what he saw, and asked fashion photographer Barry Lategan to take some pictures, which he hung in the salon. These were spotted by another client – *Daily Express* fashion journalist Deirdre McSherry. A meeting with Twiggy was arranged, more pictures were taken and the *Express* ran a two-page story in February in which Twiggy was called 'The Face of '66.' She was 'the Cockney kid with a face to launch a thousand shapes. And she's only 16'.

The following year Piri Halasz mentioned that Twiggy was a regular at Raphael and Leonard in *A Swinger's Guide to London*. She added that 'Susan or Wanda' were 'excellent,' and that the price of styling, shampoo and set was £2 16s 6d. Raphael and Leonard's big-name clients included Jackie Kennedy, Mick Jagger and Terence Stamp. Leonard also did some hair-styling work in a number of Stanley Kubrick movies, but his career was effectively ended by a brain tumour in 1988. Justin de Villeneuve and Twiggy went their separate ways in 1973.

## No. 23 Brook Street

## London, W1K 4HB

The top floor flat in this building was the home of Jimi Hendrix and his girlfriend Kathy Etchingham on and off from July 1968 until June 1969. The house next door – No. 25 – had been the residence of the German composer George Frideric Handel in the eighteenth century. The Handel House opened to the public in 2001, while the Hendrix flat part followed suit in February 2016.

Former Handel & Hendrix in London director and CEO Michelle Alland (an American in London, like Hendrix) says that the Handel plaque was already on the building's exterior wall when Hendrix moved in. This prompted him to ask, 'Who's this Handel cat?' and to head up to HMV on Oxford Street and buy three vinyl LP recordings of his work. Hendrix also enjoyed visits from classical musicians who went there to pay homage to the great composer. He jammed with

No. 23 Brook Street.

them, even though they didn't know who he was. And he believed that he once saw Handel's ghost in the flat's bathroom mirror.

Hendrix also jammed with the likes of George Harrison, Eric Clapton and Steve Winwood during his time at Brook Street. The neighbours seldom complained as there were very few of them in what was then primarily a commercial district. Brook Street was a place where Hendrix and Etchingham liked to unwind. Alland says that Etchingham, who lives in Australia, has suggested that Brook Street was probably far wilder in Handel's day when operatic 'prima donnas' went there for rehearsal. It was a 'mad house' with candelabras being thrown out of the window.

Etchingham and Hendrix gradually drifted apart and broke up in April 1969. On Sunday 29 June Hendrix wrote a note (he was at the Denver Pop Festival at the time) authorising the removal of his possessions from No. 23 Brook Street.

# Kasmin Ltd
# No. 118 New Bond Street
# London, W1S 1EW

John Kasmin ran a gallery here from 1963 until 1972. Although it was never quite as cool as the Robert Fraser Gallery, it was its main rival and the two stood out, along with Indica, in an otherwise

Kasmin Ltd.

conservative art scene. Like Fraser, Kasmin offered colourful opening shows for his artists, who included his main discovery, David Hockney.

Kasmin was born to a Jewish family in London in 1934 but grew up in Oxford. He dropped out of Magdalen College School at the age of sixteen and spent his bar mitzvah money travelling to New Zealand where he led a beatnik existence before returning to London in 1956. He got a job at the Marlborough Gallery, where he met a wealthy Oxford undergraduate, Sheridan Dufferin (real name: Sheridan Hamilton-Temple-Blackwood), the 5th Marquess of Dufferin and Ava, who would provide the financial backing for the gallery.

## Vidal Sassoon
## No. 171 New Bond Street
## London, W1S 4RD

This was the location of Vidal Sassoon's hair salon from 1959 onwards. The exact chronology isn't clear, but at some stage either before or after that the Swinging London look was born (or at least conceived) when Sassoon first cut the hair of fashion designer (and miniskirt inventor) Mary Quant. Voguepedia says that this encounter took place in 1957, while Shawn Levy's book *Ready, Steady, Go! Swinging London and the Invention of Cool* places it in 1963.

In an article published in *The Daily Mail* on Sassoon's death in 2012, Quant says that it happened 'one day in the early Sixties'. In the same piece she hailed Sassoon as 'a formative figure' of that decade, 'along with the Pill and the miniskirt, his influence was truly liberating'. And, as she told Sassoon himself (in the 2010 documentary *Vidal Sassoon: The Movie*), 'I made the clothes, but you put the top on.'

In any case, Sassoon's short hairstyles ('the bob cut,' and later 'the five-point' cut) were taken up by other famous women in the 1960s. They included the actress Nancy Kwan (in the 1963 film, *The Wild Affair*, which according to IMDB was the first time that the Swinging London look was captured on film), the singer Cilla Black and the model (and later *Vogue* editor) Grace Coddington.

Sassoon's empire began to expand and in 1965 he opened a salon in New York. This caught the attention of Ira Levin, who mentioned the stylist in his 1967 bestseller *Rosemary's Baby*, and this was repeated in Roman Polanski's 1968 film version, which starred Mia Farrow with very short hair.

Vidal Sassoon.

# W1: MARYLEBONE

## The Speakeasy
## Nos 48–50 Margaret Street
## London, W1W 85E

The Speakeasy opened in late 1966 and, according to Stash de Rola, it went on to replace the Scotch of St James as the in crowd's favourite hang-out. Simon Nicol of Fairport Convention recalls:

> We used to play at the Speakeasy on a fairly regular basis, like every fortnight or so. The Speakeasy was an after-hours nightclub popular with the industry, you know, the fashion and music and media world, and there was a band there every night and we were sort of one of that circuit of groups that passed through their doors, and there was a young American guitarist who used to get up and sit in with us because he couldn't stop himself from playing the guitar. So sometimes I'd take off my guitar and give it to Jimi Hendrix, sit back and listen. It was cool.

Probably Hendrix's most famous performance at the Speakeasy was a 30-minute rendition of 'Auld Lang's Syne' on New Year's Eve in 1967. A few months later, in the early summer of 1968, David

The Speakeasy.

Bowie first met Angie at the Speakeasy, while about a year earlier (Monday 15 May 1967) the club had witnessed the birth of another famous rock 'n' roll romance, when Paul MCartney went there with Linda Eastman after having met her at the nearby Bag O'Nails. As Paul recalls in *The Beatles Anthology*, it was at the Speakeasy that night that he first heard Procol Harum's 'A Whiter Shade of Pale'. He – and everybody else – assumed the song was by Steve Winwood.

Brian Auger saw Procol Harum play live at the Speakeasy:

After a while people were just given their own night, so we had Monday nights with the Trinity, and I remember some band coming in, you know, and somebody said, 'You want to watch these guys, they've got this single's just come out called A Whiter Shade of Pale.' I said, 'Oh, really?' And we were all on about 25 quid a night in this place, and about three weeks later, this, you know, this record comes out and Bam! It goes to number one worldwide, so I think they got a little bit more than 25 quid when they went out after that!

Jenny Fabian recalls:

After *Groupie* came out I started to have an affair with Tony Howard, who was the manager of the Speakeasy. He was a really, really nice guy; unfortunately, not with us anymore. Anyway, he was the manager there, and so I now had carte blanche to come in and out as I wanted. I could always get a seat at the restaurant. I mean, getting into the Speakeasy was one thing, but getting into the inner sanctum of the restaurant was another. And you'd sit down and eat peppered steaks and drink lots of vodka and see lots of famous people, and maybe even get off with some of them, except I wasn't supposed to because I was with Tony!

Jenny Fabian's book *Groupie* was published in 1969 – the same year that Deep Purple made their debut at the Speakeasy. The band's bass guitarist Roger Glover agrees that the food was good:

Apart from having a good restaurant, which it did, our main meal of the day used to be at 2 o'clock in the morning in those days, that was the rock'n'roll life, but it was the kind of place where Hendrix would go, Jeff Beck would go, people would get up and jam, it was actually the real kind of watering hole of a lot of the bands of that time, and it changed. I mean, later on, musicians didn't go there any more, it was all sort of roadies and stuff, but back in '69, that was the place, yes.

Deep Purple's lead singer Ian Gillan adds:

It was a hot place. I mean all the musicians and the journos used to hang out there and the liggers. Good bar; it was like a speakeasy in the days of prohibition in America. Things were going on there that you couldn't get away with in other places! The night that we played there, our opening show with Deep Purple, I looked at Rog and I [thought], 'This is it, this what I've always wanted, the band is perfect, but we were surrounded by our contemporaries and our peers, it wasn't a regular audience in there, it was an audience that was inside music, and we got phenomenal encouragement from that.

The Speak's reputation as a hangout for musicians, media and fashion industry types attracted the attention of people from other walks of life. According to Stash de Rola: 'And one night I got to the Speakeasy, and they wouldn't let in this very good-looking girl, and she was furious, and I was about to say something, and she said, 'And you'll be sorry you refused Christine Keeler!"

No. 34 Montague Square.

## No. 34 Montague Square
## London, W1H 2LJ

A blue plaque informs us that 'John Lennon 1940–1980 musician and writer lived here in 1968', but that is only part of the story. Ringo Starr originally rented a ground-floor apartment in this Grade II listed 1810 building in 1965, prior to marrying Maureen Cox and moving in 1966. He then sublet it to Paul McCartney, who used it as a home studio, and then to Jimi Hendrix and Chas Chandler. It later became the home of John Lennon and Yoko Ono, after John had left Cynthia, Julian and Weybridge. It was here that John and Yoko posed naked in October 1968 for the cover of *Unfinished Music No. 1: Two Virgins*. Later that month the police raided the apartment and John and Yoko were busted for possession of cannabis. Ringo Starr cancelled his contract with the landlord in February 1969.

## No. 57 Wimpole Street
## London, W1G 8YW

Paul McCartney lived here as a guest of the parents of his then girlfriend, Jane Asher, from late 1963 to early 1966. Jane's father, Richard (Dr R. A. J. Asher) was a distinguished physician who was in charge of the 'mental observation unit' at Central Middlesex Hospital, in addition to having private consulting rooms at the house. He wrote papers for medical journals on such subjects as 'The Dangers of Going to Bed' and 'Why Are Medical Journals So Dull?'. Jane's mother, Margaret (née Eliot), on the other hand, was an oboe teacher at the Guildhall School of Music and Drama, where her students had included future Beatles producer George Martin. According to (Barry) Miles's book *In the Sixties*, she also taught Paul to play the recorder (which would come in handy for 'Fool on the Hill'). Jane's brother, Peter, was part of the Peter and Gordon duo, for whom Paul penned 'A World Without Love' (although John shared the writing credits). Later Peter would become part of the MAD triumvirate (along with Barry Miles, or 'Miles', and Marianne Faithfull's husband, John Dunbar) which founded Indica. He would also work for Apple, where he discovered James Taylor, whom he would later manage in the United States. A sister, Clare Asher, who had an acting career prior to becoming a schoolteacher, also lived at No. 57 Wimpole Street.

No. 57 Wimpole Street.

Jane was herself a successful actress and she first met Paul at a show at the Albert Hall in April 1963. Miles describes Richard Asher as something of an eccentric who liked to perform odd jobs around the house in the small hours of the morning dressed in a blue boiler suit. Paul and Peter lived on the top floor, while the music room – Richard was also musical – was in the basement. It was here that John and Paul wrote 'I Wanna Hold Your Hand', and that Paul composed 'Yesterday', the melody for which had come to him in a dream. It was also during his time at Wimpole Street that Paul received a letter from his accountant, Harry Pinkser, who informed him: 'I thought you might like to know that technically you are a millionaire.'

# The Apple Shop
# No. 94 Baker Street
# London, W1U 6FZ

This was the location of the Apple Shop (John Lennon having vetoed the word 'Boutique'), a short-lived Beatle enterprise. It opened for business on Thursday 7 December 1967 and closed on Tuesday 30 July 1968. As a clothes store it was off the beaten track, in addition to which it was badly managed, with both customers and staff helping themselves to stock.

The launch party on Tuesday 5 December was hosted by John and George as Paul and Ringo were out of town. Guests, who included Liverpudlian singer Cilla Black, critic Kenneth Tynan,

The Apple Shop.

DJ Alan Freeman and Beatle film director Richard Lester, were served apples (by a clown) and apple juice. The shop's basic idea was to encourage people to wear the sort of clothes that the Beatles wore, but things rapidly went awry. It was also famous for its psychedelic mural, which was designed by the Dutch design duo The Fool. The locals hated it and the council ordered its removal. It was whitewashed in May and replaced with the word 'Apple'. As John Lennon said (in a posthumous interview *The Beatles Anthology*), the venture ended up with 'all this junk and The Fool and all the stupid clothes and all that'.

The Apple Shop did, however, appear as a location in the 1968 movie *Hot Millions*, starring Peter Ustinov, Maggie Smith, Karl Malden and Bob Newhart. In one scene Bob Newhart takes Maggie Smith shopping there. He spends the princely sum of £20.

When Apple decided to close the place down the Beatles and friends went there to help themselves to whatever they wanted. The following day the general public was invited to follow suit. The result was mayhem. The Beatles' PR man Derek Taylor called the scene (in *The Beatles Anthology*) 'awful and vulgar' and described 'cabbies grabbing kaftans and capes and silk ruffled shirts off rails'.

Nor did things improve after the closure. Paul McCartney decided that the empty retail space's whitewashed windows would be the perfect place to offer some free promo for the group's forthcoming single 'Hey Jude' (which was released on Monday 26 August). He therefore scraped the words 'Hey Jude' out of the whitewash. He was somewhat surprised when a furious Jewish delicatessen owner in the neighbourhood rang him up a few hours later and threatened to send his son round to beat him up. McCartney said that he was unaware of the word Jude's associations with the Nazi era, when it was painted on the windows of Jewish-owned businesses.

# W2

## Hyde Park
## London, W2

Estimates vary as to the number of fans who attended the free concert in Hyde Park on Saturday 5 July 1969: some accounts say 250,000, others half a million. People usually refer to this massive event as 'the Stones concert', even though several other acts performed that day, including Family, King Crimson, Roy Harper, the Third Ear Band, Battered Ornaments, Alexis Korner's New Church and Screw.

The 5 July show was in fact the second in a series of free concerts in Hyde Park that summer. The first, on Saturday 7 June, featured Richie Havens (who would play at Woodstock a few weeks later), Blind Faith, Donovan, the Edgar Broughton Band and the aforementioned Third Ear Band.

It is generally thought that the concert was a tribute to former Rolling Stones guitarist Brian Jones, who had drowned in mysterious circumstances two days beforehand in the swimming pool of his Sussex home. The concert had in fact been organised several weeks previously, but the Stones turned it into a memorial. At the start of their set Jagger read a few lines from Shelley's *Adonais: An Elegy on the Death of John Keats*, which had been written 148 years previously. After the reading 3,500 butterflies were released into the air.

*Melody Maker* journalist and *Swinging London: A Guide to Where the Action Is* co-author Karl Dallas remembered:

> A very hot day, all these beautiful girls in chiffon blouses with no bras, which was very nice, and the Stones played very badly, very out of tune, but of course, again, it was the ambience, it didn't really matter because, although the Stones are great musicians, especially Keith ... it's very difficult, especially a live gig where you don't have a lot of time for doing a soundcheck, they were out of tune, terribly out of tune.

*International Times* journalist and Deviants lead singer Mick Farren described the concert in his memoir *Give the Anarchist a Cigarette*, recalling that he and his then girlfriend Germaine Greer had become a rather public item. He admitted to feeling uncomfortable at the backstage garden party, which was organised by concert promoters Blackhill Enterprises (whose name appeared on a large onstage banner). Farren went off in search of 'stimulants,' leaving Greer in the company of former boyfriend Blind Faith and one-time Cream drummer Ginger Baker. Farren also pointed out that the concert stage was at the cockpit near the Serpentine. This was in contrast to the stage at the final Hyde Park concert of 1969 on Saturday 20 September, which was held in the meadow near

Speaker's Corner. The line-up on that occasion consisted of Soft Machine, Al Stewart, Quintessence, the Edgar Broughton Band and, of course, the Deviants.

Hyde Park.

# W8

## The Trattoo
## No. 2 Abingdon Road
## London, W8 6AF

The Trattoo was part of the restaurant empire built by Mario Cassandro and Franco Lagattolla, owners of the Trattoria La Terrazza in Soho. As Alasdair Scott Sutherland explains in *The Spaghetti Tree*, they acquired the site of Les Pies Qui Rient from an anonymous Egyptian for £25,000 in December 1966. They installed Pasquale Lunghi, a headwaiter at the Tratt, as manager and spent £1,500 on a lavish launch party a couple of months later.

The Trattoo.

The restaurant soon attracted celebrities. Barry Fantoni recalls: 'Spike Milligan lived close to the Trattoo. I often ate there with him when he was feeling well.' Milligan's fellow Goon Peter Sellers was also a regular, as was the actor Richard Harris, about whom Alasdair Scott Sutherland says:

Mrs Harris, Elizabeth Harris, who had been already been married to Rex Harrison, turns up at the front door, to be told 'Yes, of course,' her table is ready, but they've forgotten that her current husband, Richard Harris, is there with another woman downstairs. So Pasquale told me he had to go running down, grab Richard Harris, take him out the back way through the men's lavatories while he seated his current wife Elizabeth with her new boyfriend. By this time Harris, of course, had had rather too much to drink, as he did most nights in those days, and he then comes round the front again and demands to be let in because he hasn't finished his drink!

Other Trattoo regulars included photographers Brian Duffy, David Bailey and his wife Catherine Deneuve and her fellow actors Christopher Plummer and Oliver Reed. Robert Vaughn once dined there in a Nazi uniform, apparently as part of his preparation for his role as Major Paul Kreuger in the 1969 film *The Bridge at Remagen*.

# Biba 1
# No. 87 Abingdon Rd
# London, W8 6AW

Biba was a major player in the 1960s fashion world, providing groovy yet affordable clothes for the nation's teenage girls, who at that time included Princess Anne. The shop was set up by Barbara Hulanicki, who had moved to Brighton aged twelve in 1948 after her Polish diplomat father had been assassinated in Jerusalem. His young widow and three daughters then moved to London.

Barbara Hulanicki began her professional career as a fashion illustrator but discovered that her talents could be put to better use as a fashion designer. She and her business partner (and husband) Stephen Fitz-Simmon started selling clothes by mail order, but they were so successful that they decided to open a shop. 'Biba' was in fact the diminutive of Biruta, the name of Barbara Hulanicki's sister.

As Hulanicki relates in her autobiography, *From A to Biba*, she took to driving around London and found 'marvelous dilapidated corner premises' in Abingdon Road owned by an Irishman called Mr O'Grady. The shop opened for business in 1964, but its stock quickly sold out. The fact that *Ready, Steady, Go!* presenter Cathy McGowan was a client certainly helped. She regularly wore a new Biba outfit on the show on Friday night and girls flocked to the store to get their copies the following morning.

Other clients at Abingdon Road included Sonny and Cher, photographer Richard Avedon, Mick Jagger and his then girlfriend Chrissie Shrimpton, and 'a lovely skinny girl' called Lesley Hornby, who later became Twiggy. In *A to B*, Barbara Hulanicki also relates that they received a visit from a 'tiny blonde girl' who, prior to trying on clothes, stripped off in the middle of the shop. It turned out to be Julie Christie who, Hulanicki reckons, was trying out clothes for the film *Darling* (which was released in 1965).

No. 87 Abingdon Road was also on the diminutive side for the shop's huge clientele and it moved to larger premises at Nos 19–21 Kensington Church Street (a former grocers) in March 1966 (although some accounts say the move took place in late 1965). According to Shawn Levy's book, *Ready, Steady, Go! Swinging London and the Invention of Cool*, it proved to be an excellent publicity stunt. A removal van was hired with Cathy MacGowan, Cilla Black (another client) and assorted Biba girls hanging on the back.

The Biba logo.

Biba 1.

## Biba 2

## Nos 19–21 Kensington Church Street

## London, W8 4LF

Biba moved here from No. 87 Abingdon Road in March 1966. Its continued popularity is chronicled in three guidebooks from 1967. In *Len Deighton's London Dossier* Drusilla Beyfus says that it is 'noted for inexpensive bang-on-now fashion and accessories,' while Piri Halasz's *A Swinger's Guide to London* observes that 'it draws young things (and their beaux) from all over London,' and Dallas and Fantoni's *Swinging London A Guide to Where the Action Is* informs us that on Friday night and Saturday morning 'the archetypal dollies flock to Biba to see what goodies Barbara Hulanicki has got for them this week'. It also lists the hours – 9.30 to 8 p.m. (Thursday 1 p.m.), Saturday 9.30 a.m. to 5.30 p.m. – and prices – 1*s* to £15.

Biba 2.

# Biba 3
## No. 120 Kensington High Street
## London, W8 6SU

This was the location of the third Biba store: the company moved to this former carpet shop in September 1969. As Barbara Hulanicki recalls in *From A to Biba*, the most dramatic event was the planting of a bomb by the Angry Brigade on 1 May 1971. It would move to its final premises, 'Big Biba,' at the art deco Derry & Toms building at No. 99 High Street, Kensington, in September 1973, before closing in 1975.

Biba 3.

# W10

## I Was Lord Kitchener's Valet
## No. 293 Portobello Road
## London, W10 5TD

This was the original location of I Was Lord Kitchener's Valet, a shop that specialised in Victorian military uniforms. Like Granny Takes a Trip, it was the subject of a song, recorded by the New Vaudeville Band (who were also responsible for the international hit Winchester Cathedral) in 1967 (the same year as the Purple Gang's Granny Takes a Trip).

I Was Lord Kitchener's Valet.

The shop had begun life as a stall on Portobello Market in 1964 before acquiring more stable premises in 1966. It was owned by Ian Fish and John Paul while Robert Orbach, who had previously worked for John Stephen, 'the King of Carnaby Street,' was a director. In an interview for the Victoria & Albert Museum in 2006, Orbach recalled: 'I'm sitting there one morning and in walked John Lennon, Mick Jagger and Cynthia Lennon. And I didn't know whether I was hallucinating… but it was real.' Jagger bought a floral red Grenadier Guards drummer's jacket 'probably for about £4 to £5' (along with the rest of the shop's stock, it had been acquired at either Moss Bros or British Army Surplus). He wore it on *Ready, Steady, Go!* when the Stones played 'Paint it Black' (the song was released in May 1966 but the band performed it on the show on Friday 7 October). Orbach said, 'The next morning there was a line of about 100 people wanting to buy this tunic… and we sold everything in the shop by lunchtime.' Other devotees of the store's military tunics included Eric Clapton and Jimi Hendrix.

The success of I Was Lord Kitchener's Valet was such that branches were opened in 1967 at more central locations: Piccadilly Circus and Foubert's Place (very near Orbach's old stomping ground of Carnaby Street). There was also an I Was Lord Kitchener's Thing on the King's Road.

Fish and Paul ended their business relationship in 1967. Fisk took over No. 293 Portobello Road and changed the name to the Injun Dog, a 'head shop'.

# W11

## The Jazz Record Store
## No. 209 Westbourne Park Road
## London, W11 1EA

In his memoir *Give the Anarchist a Cigarette* Mick Farren described a jazz record store that had been set up in the early 1960s by two significant members of the underground scene, namely Alexander Trocchi and Michael de Freitas. Trocchi (1925–84), who was from Glasgow (although his father was Italian), was a novelist, poet, heroin addict and friend of William Burroughs. De Freitas (1933–75), who was from Trinidad (although his father was Portuguese), had arrived in London in 1957 and had worked as an enforcer for the notorious Notting Hill landlord Peter Rachman (1919–62). He later became an activist, changing his name first to Abdul Malik and then

The Jazz
Record Store.

to Michael X. He returned to Trinidad in 1971, where he was hanged in 1975 for the 1972 murder of Joseph Skerritt. As has been chronicled in the film *The Bank Job*, Michael X was also charged with the murder of Gale Benson, the daughter of the Conservative MP Leonard Plugge, although he was never tried.

Some accounts place the record store in Powis Square, but in *Give the Anarchist a Cigarette* Mick Farren said it was on Westbourne Park Road, while in Jonathon Green's oral history *Days in the Life*, Farren said it was on Ledbury Road. The Safari Tent stood at No. 207 Westbourne Park Road, on the north-east corner of Ledbury Road. It's possible – but by no means certain – that the store was on the opposite corner at No. 209.

Michael X's friends and sponsors included John Lennon and Yoko Ono, but his fellow Trinidadian and activist Darcus Howe was less impressed: 'Michael X was a semi-literate liar and a thief. He was a hustler, a pimp, and once he heard about Malcolm – his name was Michael de Freitas – he put an X next to his name. He was a hustler. He and Trocchi were shooting heroin together.'

Howe added: 'And also he's half-white, half-Portuguese, his father was a man who had a shop and his mother used to go to buy sugar, and the man fucked her and then he came, so he was seen as higher in the society than black boys like myself.'

Howe concluded: 'He wanted to go to jail, and if you talked any organisational business with him, all he talks about is money. He was terrific, a thief. He wanted to kill me one time, I said: "Tell him that's a sure way to commit suicide! Come!"'

# The Safari Tent

# No. 207 Westbourne Park Road

# London, W11 1EA

Mick Farren went to live in the Notting Hill-Ladbroke Grove area in the early 1960s. He later recalled:

> I moved there just after the kind of the Colin MacInnes time and the Teddy Boy riots and, really, there were the old kind of illegal shebeens, which kind of linked into the Profumo Scandal, Lucky Gordon, Christine Keeler, there was those joints. There was the Safari Tent, which was a Jamaican restaurant, where you could kind of get a drink under the counter, which was reasonably safe and reasonably friendly.

Trinidadian Darcus Howe, on the other hand, didn't frequent the Safari Tent, as he 'preferred Chinese food back then'.

Mick Farren had more about the Safari Tent in his memoir *Give the Anarchist a Cigarette*, saying that it was run by 'a West Indian with a Harry Belafonte lilt called Johnny Millington,' and that it was frequented by Swedish au pairs and rude boys.

Notting Hill has undergone considerable gentrification since then. Lexicographer Jonathon Green, who worked as a journalist with the *International Times*, misses the good old days: 'It was much poorer. I mean, I'm not there enough, but I presume it was much blacker, it was much more interesting. It was a wonderful place, where you could get a joint 24/7, wherever you were!'

The Safari Tent was at No. 207 Westbourne Park Road (opposite the Jazz Record Store at No. 209), but the building appears to have been demolished to make way for the lawn that stands in front of Wessex Gardens, a block of flats.

The Safari Tent.

## El Rio Cafe
## No. 127 Westbourne Park Road
## London, W11 5QL
## Underground: Notting Hill Gate, Westbourne Park

When Darcus Howe arrived in London as a young man in 1962, the Rio was his first point of call: 'And I went in the basement. It was Frank's [Crichlow] place, it was called the Rio coffee bar.' Clients included 'MacInnes, Christine Keeler before she was known. So there's a little bit of whoring going on, and a little bit of, you know, "discovering the negro!" And in the basement they played dice and cards. The dice game was Parapinto and the card game was a kind of gin rummy with 14 cards. That came from Jamaica.'

The Rio had been opened by Darcus Howe's fellow Trinidadian Frank Crichlow in 1959, the same year that Colin MacInnes had published his novel *Absolute Beginners*, which described the Notting Hill/Teddy Boy riots of 1958. As Darcus Howe said, MacInnes was a regular at the Rio, but for art student Mick Farren, who arrived in London around the same time as Howe (from an admittedly less exotic native heath, Sussex), it was a daunting place, rather less friendly to white boys than the nearby Safari: 'And a few blocks on down Westbourne Park Road there was the Rio, which was kind of notorious, and, you know, you could score a quarter of grass in there, but you kind of took your life in your hands. Well, I guess today they'd be rudies, but they looked like grown men to us at the time and, you know, some very sort of sinister kind of Ray Charles shades, Charlie Mingus-looking guys.'

Darcus Howe agreed that the Grove in those days was not a place for the faint-hearted: 'The detritus, the pimps, ponces, all kinds of things. And then you'll see all these West Indians going to

El Rio Café.

church on a Sunday morning, with their prayer books and their children. And on the other hand when darkness fell on the wings of the night, all sorts are taking place, pimps, all sorts!'

Frank Crichlow described the Rio as 'a school or university' for hustlers. Not surprisingly perhaps, it attracted the likes of MacInnes and Christine Keeler, who went there (according to Richard Davenport-Hines's book *An English Affair: Sex, Class and Power in The Age of Profumo*) in October 1961 with Stephen Ward. It was at the Rio that she met another member of the Profumo cast, Jamaican musician Aloysius 'Lucky' Gordon.

## No. 25 Powis Square
## London, W11 2AZ

No. 25 Powis Square appeared in one of the great '60s London movies, namely *Performance*, which was shot in 1968, but not released until 1970 as its contents were considered too shocking by its distributors, Warner Bros. Co-directed by Donald Cammell and Nicholas Roeg, it centred around a gangster on the run, Chas (James Fox), and his bizarre relationship with a rock star, Turner (Mick Jagger), and his two live-in girlfriends, Pherber (Anita Pallenberg) and Lucy (Michele Breton). Chas moves into their strange abode, prior to being tracked down by his colleagues from the underworld.

The house in question was No. 25 Powis Square, even though it was only used for the exterior scenes. The interior drama was filmed at a house in Lowndes Square.

According to Mick Farren, *Performance* was the perfect expression of the coming together of different social groups in Swinging London; criminals like the Kray Twins, rock stars and the aristocracy, who started going to the same parties: 'There was a kind of nexus of serious gangsters, the young, rather sort of effete Aubrey Beardsley aristocratic wastrels, the Rolling Stones, Eric Burdon. A lot of it kind of coalesced around the making of *Performance*, and Nicolas Roeg and Donald Cammell and hints of black magic and whatever.'

The hints of black magic may have been too much for James Fox who abandoned his acting career about a year after the release of *Performance* in order to become an evangelical Christian. According to Alexander Walker's book *Hollywood England: The British Film Industry in the Sixties*, he joined The Navigators and started spreading the word of God in the Midlands. He returned to acting in the 1980s.

No. 25 Powis Square.

# The London Free School
# No. 26 Powis Terrace
# London, W11 1JH

The London Free School (LFS) offered 'Free education through lectures and discussion groups in subjects essential to our daily life and work.' It came into existence at a public meeting on Tuesday 8 March 1966. It was the brainchild of John Hopkins, aka Hoppy (1937–2015), while local community activist Rhaune Laslett became president. Its premises, in the basement of No. 26 Powis Terrace, had previously been used by Michael X as a gambling club. According to (Barry) Miles's book *London Calling*, Michael X's landlord, John Michell, was delighted when his tenant decided to use it for a more educational project. Michell even gave classes in UFOs and ley lines. According to Anjelica Huston, it was in the basement of a fish and chip shop. She was an American teenager in London at the time, thanks to her father John's work as a film director. She was officially a pupil at Holland Park School but preferred to play truant and hang out at the LFS.

The London Free School.

# W12

## HM Prison Wormwood Scrubs
## DuCane Road
## London, W12 0AE

Not only was HM Prison Wormwood Scrubs used as a location in several famous Swinging London movies, it also featured in some significant real life events.

We see the prison's famous Victorian entrance in John Schlesinger's *Billy Liar* (1963). Billy, played by Tom Courteney, lives in a fantasy world and in one sequence he is released from the prison as a hero. The entrance also appears in *Morgan: A Suitable Case for Treatment*, a Karel Reisz comedy that was released in January 1966.

It was also in 1966 that student James Clough served a one-month sentence at 'the Scrubs' after being arrested during the anti-Vietnam War demonstration at the US Embassy on Sunday 3 July. It was, he says:

> Quite traumatic for me. We arrived there. I can remember the changing room, taking off all your clothes in front of the guards: it was terrifying. Handing in all your belongings and putting them in a little box, wearing a prison uniform, YP [Young Prisoner] followed by a number. It was very grim. I think there were four if us in a cell, a few Irish kids. I have memories of slopping out, memories of the awful food, memories of the World Cup because it was July 1966 and Wembley was only a very short distance away, so we could actually hear what was going on and hear that England was winning. Of course, there was no television in prison at that time. That was one of the high points of that month! Everybody had some kind of work or another and most of the prisoners painted plastic Noddies! I don't know how I got exempted from that, but they put me in the library, if you could call it a library: it was a tiny room with a few tattered books. The chief librarian was a lifer. I don't know what he'd done: he must have killed somebody. He was an RAF man, and we got on quite well.

And, like Billy Liar, James Clough was happy to leave Wormwood Scrubs: 'The last day, savouring what was going to be freedom, was just a wonderful emotion for me. It was absolutely, overwhelmingly joyful, especially that summer. Feeling the heat and the sunshine was marvellous: I hadn't seen it for a month as there were no outdoor possibilities at Wormwood Scrubs.'

The film *Morgan*, on the other hand, tells the story of Morgan Delt, a failed working-class artist (played by David Warner), who is sent to prison after abducting his estranged upper-middle-class wife Leonie (played by Vanessa Redgrave). Morgan and his mother (played by Irene Handl) are both ardent communists and it is therefore ironic that a few months after the film's release Soviet

HM Prison Wormwood Scrubs.

double agent George Blake, who was five years into a forty-two-year sentence, would make a dramatic escape from Wormwood Scrubs (on Saturday 22 October 1966), eventually reaching East Berlin and later Moscow. Blake's time in prison coincided with that of Michael Hollingshead, 'the man who turned on the world'. Hollingshead is alleged to have smuggled some tabs of acid into Wormwood Scrubs and to have given at least one of them to Blake.

In *Morgan* the main character loses his wife to Charles Napier (played by Robert Stephens), an aristocratic art gallery owner who seems to be a heterosexual version of Robert Fraser. And so there is also a certain irony in the fact that Robert Fraser would spend six months at Wormwood Scrubs the following year. This was after the police raid on Keith Richards' Sussex home, Redlands. Richards was given a one-year sentence (on Thursday 29 June 1967), but only spent one night in 'the Scrubs,' being released the following day, even though he admitted in his autobiography *Life* that he 'didn't enjoy' his 24 hours there. Fraser, on the other hand, who was 'sent down' for six months, felt at home in 'the Scrubs.' He had plenty of boyfriends and in those class-conscious days an Old Etonian army officer was looked up to by inmates and guards alike. The guards even began to wait on him, like butlers. Fraser later said prison was 'just like being back at Eton'.

The toffs were also respected in Peter Collinson's film *The Italian Job*, which was released on Monday 2 June 1969. The most important person in the prison is an inmate, Mr Bridger (played by Noel Coward), who reprimands the governor when an outsider, Charlie Croker (played by Michael Caine), infiltrates the toilet cubicles when he is using one of them. The prison's exterior was used as a location in the film, although the interior scenes were shot at Kilmainham Jail in Dublin.

# The Massacre of Braybrook Street
# (Opposite) No. 61 Braybrook Street
# London, W12 0AL

On Braybrook Street, a few hundred yards from Wormwood Scrubs prison, there is a tombstone-like plaque. It is near the spot where on Friday 12 August 1966 three unarmed police officers – PS Christopher Head, PC Geoffrey Fox and PC David Wombwell – were shot and killed by Harry Roberts and his accomplices, Jack Witney and John Duddy.

The episode, which took place less than a fortnight after the England's World Cup final victory at Wembley, was known as both the 'Massacre of Braybrook Street' and the 'Shepherd's Bush

Braybrook Street.

Murders'. It led to a national outpouring of anger and grief, and the three slain officers were later honoured with a memorial service at Westminster Abbey. Many people called for the reinstatement of capital punishment, which had been abolished in Britain the previous year. Witney and Duddy were arrested within a week of the massacre, but Roberts, who had learned survival techniques as a soldier in Malayan jungle in the 1950s, stayed on the run for three months. He was finally found in a barn at Blount's Farm, near Bishop's Stortford, on Tuesday 15 November.

In the meantime, the massive manhunt had been temporarily eclipsed in the media by the escape of Soviet spy George Blake from Wormwood Scrubs on 22 October. Roberts and Blake had known each other inside 'the Scrubs' and there was even a theory that Roberts had masterminded Blake's escape. Roberts was taken back to Wormwood Scrubs shortly after his arrest and was released from prison in November 2014.

The plaque stands on the edge of the Wormwood Scrubs Nature Reserve, across the road from No. 61 Braybrook Street.

# W14

## No. 11 Gunterstone Road
## London, W14 9BP

Zoot Money (leader of Zoot Money's Big Roll Band, and a session man with many other groups) lived in a flat here in the 1960s and it was a popular hangout for his fellow musicians. Brian Auger provides a few names:

> Brian Jones, from the Stones, when he actually left the Stones and all sorts of other people, guys from The Animals, Eric Burdon, and we would just play records all night and hang out, and Jimi [Hendrix] eventually had a flat just above there that he moved into. So this was one of those kind of fraternity things, and we all had a good laugh. [Future Police guitarist – ed.] Andy Summers, another one, who was in Zoot's band: a great player, man!

No. 11 Gunterstone Road.

The flat was located at Baron's Court, in west London, and this proved convenient. According to rock legend, when Jimi Hendrix first landed at Heathrow Airport in September 1966, his manager (former Animal) Chas Chadler immediately took him to Gunterstone Road, where he allegedly jammed with Zoot Money and Andy Summers. Summers has, however, said in interviews that he didn't meet Hendrix until a few days later.

No. 11 Gunterstone Road was also the home of Kathy Etchingham, who would soon become Hendrix's girlfriend. Her middle name was Mary and she is thought to have been the inspiration for the song 'The Wind Cries Mary'.

As for Brian Jones, he wasn't officially fired from the Rolling Stones until a few weeks before his death on 3 July 1969, but, as Keith Richards says in his autobiography, *Life*, Jones ceased to be an effective member of the group around 1966, so the chronology fits Brian Auger's account.

# WC1

## The Indica Bookshop and *International Times*
## No. 102 Southampton Row
## London, WC1B 4BL

The Indica bookshop moved to No. 102 Southampton Row in the summer of 1966. It had previously shared premises with the gallery of the same name at No. 6 Mason's Yard. The bookshop occupied the ground floor at Southampton Row, while in October of that year the basement became the editorial offices of the underground newspaper *International Times* (*IT*). (Barry) Miles, who was one of the founders of all three ventures, even took a flat (with his then wife Sue) at No. 106 Southampton Row. Several decades later he explained the paper's basic idea:

> People like Hoppy [co-founder John Hopkins, 1937–2017 – ed.] and I were looking around thinking, 'There is a real constituency of people here who are not represented at all,' which is why we began the *International Times*, the first underground paper in Europe, which was to cater for these people. It wasn't supposed to be a revolutionary paper or anything, it was really just a way of introducing information that you couldn't get from the straight press because in those days you couldn't just start a newspaper or go and write for *The Observer*, you had to do your two years' apprenticeship on the *Brighton & Hove Argus* or something. You know, it was all very, very cumbersome, and then you had to be in the union. It would probably have been more of a straight paper, had it not been for the unions and the rules and all that. So we had to make it an underground paper, it was the only way we could do it; it was outside of normal society.

As Miles states in his book, *In the Sixties*, the first issue of *IT* was published on Friday 14 October. The launch party, which had taken place five days earlier at the Roundhouse, was one of the great '60s events. It certainly helped identify *IT* with the underground. As Miles says:

> And we just wanted to show people what was going on in the arts and in poetry and in experimental literature and this, that and the other, and what made it into a really underground paper was that we also just simply reported on the price of drugs, even though they were illegal. We didn't comment on them, we didn't say they should be legalised, we just said hash costs whatever it was! And also, if there were some well-known police informers, we'd describe them as well.

The Indica Bookshop and
*International Times.*

This could explain why the police raided the *IT* offices on Thursday 9 March 1967, a few days after the first raid on Middle Earth, and a few weeks after their visit to Keith Richards' Sussex home, Redlands. The officers at *IT* were allegedly searching for pornographic material. Miles recalls:

> But, boy did they come down on us! I mean, we got busted within six issues or something, and every single piece of paper in the office was taken away, even the phone books, and people's personal address books, their pay cheques, everything was taken away, and kept for four months, and then returned without any charges being made. It would have closed down absolutely any other organisation, except an underground newspaper. First of all, the UFO Club was up and running by then so we turned it into a theatrical piece, where all of the copy for the next issue was read aloud as a theatre piece and in fact we were only a week late before we found another printer and managed to get the thing out, and obviously we'd lost all the subscription lists and all the advertisers and had no idea how much money was owed to us etc. etc., but it was a pretty heavy response on the part of the establishment to what was basically an arts magazine covering reviews of quite intellectual shows.

As Miles says in *In the Sixties*, the Porn Squad raid was absurd, given that real pornography could be found in abundance only a few hundred yards away in Soho. It would later emerge (in a 1976 corruption trial) that the police were being paid off by the porn shops.

    *IT* began life with the Roundhouse event, and its near death led to another legendary gathering: the 14-hour Technicolour Dream at Alexandra Palace on Saturday 29 April 1967, which was essentially a benefit event for the beleaguered paper.

# The Architectural Association
# School of Architecture
# Nos 34–36 Bedford Square
# London, WC1B 3ES

This building, which forms parts of a terrace on the west side of Bedford Square, was the scene of a minor, but interesting, event in 1965. For many people London's underground scene was born at the famous International Poetry Incarnation at the Royal Albert Hall on Friday 11 June 1965.

The Architectural Association.

But, as one of its organisers, (Barry) Miles, says, 'As a poetry reading, it wasn't great!' This was in marked contrast to: 'A reading that I put on about a week later at the Architectural Association.' The cast consisted of

> Allen Ginsberg, Gregory Corso, Lawrence Ferlinghetti and Andrei Voznesensky, and all four of them read brilliantly to an audience of about 100 people and the atmosphere there was fantastic, just beautiful. And I made a record of it, actually. I recorded it and we did 99 copies of it: if you did more than 100 you had to pay purchase tax, and so we just kept it as a little limited edition thing, but that was great, really, really great.

Incidentally, Voznesensky (1933–2010) had studied architecture, prior to becoming a poet.

# WC2

## The LSE
## Houghton Street
## London, WC2A 2AE

The London School of Economics and Political Science (LSE) made two contributions to the story of the 1960s. The first was that Mick Jagger studied finance and accounting there from 1961 to 1963, but dropped out in order to pursue a career with the Rolling Stones. The second was that it was the scene of student protests later in the decade.

The first signs of trouble came with a student sit-in during March 1967, but the situation became more heated after the student riots in Paris in May 1968. The following month 500 British students gathered at the LSE to form the Revolutionary Socialist Student Federation. Noted leftists like

The LSE.

Tariq Ali and (journalist and *Private Eye* contributor) Paul Foot attended, although they did not speak, while a representative of the Black Power movement asked the audience: 'How many people sitting here know how to make a petrol bomb?'

The LSE was occupied again in October, and this led to a showdown with the authorities. Steel gates were placed at the entrance to the main buildings and students tore these down on Friday 24 January 1969. At this point the LSE's director, Walter Adam, closed the school down. A few days later the rebels set up an 'LSE in exile' at another London University building, the University of London Union (ULU) in Malet Street. The LSE reopened in March and assorted students and lecturers were expelled.

The protests received some coverage in LSE graduate Bernard Levin's 1970 book, *The Pendulum Years*. He noted that student protests also took place at Bristol and – more famously – Essex, and that one person died during the troubles at the LSE: the poor fellow was a porter who, Levin claimed, suffered from a weak heart.

The LSE has been in existence since 1895, when it was founded by Fabian socialists such as Sidney and Beatrice Webb and George Bernard Shaw, but, as Bernard Levin observed, it hadn't always been a hotbed of socialism. In the 1930s and 1940s, for example, the libertarian economist Friedrich Hayek was a lecturer there.

## The Savoy Hotel
## Strand
## London, WC2R 0EU

Bob Dylan held court here when he toured Britain in 1965. He received visits from the Beatles, Donovan, who played guitar and sang, and Marianne Faithfull, while Allen Ginsberg and Joan Baez were part of the entourage. Some of these events are chronicled in the 1967 documentary *Don't Look Back*, which features a sequence in which Dylan holds up cue cards with the lyrics to 'Subterranean Homesick Blues', as Allen Ginsberg and Bob Neuwirth silently discuss something in the background. This sequence was filmed on Saturday 8 May 1965, in an alleyway near the hotel.

The Savoy Hotel.

Marianne Faithfull describes her bizarre encounter with Dylan in her autobiography *Faithfull*.

The Beatles visited the hotel on other occasions during the decade: they attended a Variety Club lunch on Tuesday 10 September 1963 and Paul McCartney returned in July 1965 for an Ivor Novello Awards lunch.

Other guests in the 1960s included Jane Fonda, Sophia Loren and Marlon Brando. *The New London Spy* (1966) mentioned Maria Callas, Noel Coward, Charlie Chaplin, Carlo Ponti (Sophia Loren's partner) and Roger Vadim in the list of 'likely fellow guests,' adding that the hotel had 'more celebrities to the square inch of red carpet than anywhere else'. Piri Halasz (1967) placed the Savoy in 'The Famous Four' (the other three being the Connaught, the Dorchester and Claridges). She also quoted the prices: 'Singles from £7 10s, doubles from £11 10s.'

The Savoy has been associated with the entertainment industry throughout its history: it was built by the theatre impresario Richard D'Oyly Carte, allegedly with the profits from the Gilbert & Sullivan opera *The Mikado*, which played at the nearby Savoy Theatre. The hotel opened in 1889.

# The Africa Centre
# No. 38 King Street
# London, WC2E 8JS
# Underground: Covent Garden

This was the setting for the three-day 'Destruction in Art Symposium' (DIAS), which began on Friday 9 September 1966. It was organised by Gustav Metzger, who had fled from Nazi Germany as a child in the 1930s. (Barry) Miles, who describes the symposium in his book *London Calling*, recalls that the performance artists included Yoko Ono. She presented *Cut Piece*, in which she was gradually stripped naked as members of the audience were invited to come on stage and snip the clothes on her body by specially provided scissors, which were attached to contact microphones. She had first performed the work in her native Japan in 1964 and then at New York's Carnegie Hall

The Africa Centre.

in 1965. She gave her fourth and fifth performances at the Africa Centre. On other occasions, such as at the 14-Hour Technicolor Dream at Alexandra Palace (on Saturday 29 April 1967) she directed proceedings, as opposed to appearing herself. Her performances at the Africa Centre took place two months before her famous first encounter with John Lennon at the Indica Gallery.

The Africa Centre was opened by Zambian president Kenneth Kaunda in 1964. It closed in 2013 and is now located at No. 66 Suffolk Street in Southwark.

## Middle Earth
## No. 43 King Street
## London, WC2E 8JY

Middle Earth, which was named after the eponymous land in *The Lord of the Rings* and other J. R. R. Tolkien stories, rose to prominence after the demise of UFO in September 1967. According to Mick Farren's memoir, *Give the Anarchist A Cigarette*, it became the city's 'premier underground rock club'.

It was run by Dave Howson, who, according to a rumour mentioned by Farren, 'was fronting for a couple of Scottish businessmen who'd seen the hippie potential'. Jenny Fabian tends to agree:

> Dave was a sort of hippie entrepreneur. He wore the gear, the velvet jacket, the Art Deco scarf at the neck, he had a sort of mini Viva Zapata moustache, the long hair, he used to strut around in slightly raised heels, the crushed velvet trousers. He looked the part. Anyway, we started having a scene, and he was keeping me from going into work each morning. And he said, 'Stop working there and come and work for me at Middle Earth.' And I thought that sounded much more fun. So I jacked in my job at *The Daily Telegraph* magazine and became the… what was I? I was on the door at Middle Earth and also working in the office during the week.

Not surprisingly, Middle Earth appeared in Fabian's novel *Groupie*, although she changed the name to 'The Other Kingdom'. Dave Howson's assistant manager was Paul Walden. The club's main DJ was Jeff Dexter, although John Peel operated the turntable on Saturday nights. Mick Farren's group the Deviants played there, as did Soft Machine, Tomorrow, Tyrannosaurus Rex, the Graham Bond Organisation, Pink Floyd, The Who, Traffic, the Bonzo Dog Doo-Dah Band, the Incredible String Band, The Crazy World of Arthur Brown and Fairport Convention.

Judy Dyble, Fairport's first lead singer, recalled:

> It was in the basement underneath Covent Garden and during the day it was Covent Garden selling the fruit and vegetables. That was a big fruit and vegetable market where all the greengrocers went to buy their stocks from the wholesalers. At night it turned into this club which was dark, like a cavern, filthy dirty but, of course, you didn't notice it because you went in there at 10 o'clock, you played one gig at 11, one at 2, one at 4, then you came out in the early morning and I think one morning Richard [Thompson] and I came out and there was the last lamplighter in London putting out the gas lamps as the dawn came up, and that was really quite sweet.

Fellow Fairport member Simon Nicol says that 'it was a wonderful melting pot because you had these toffs coming out of the opera, literally, and it was still a working fruit and veg market, so, as the toffs were coming out, so the truck loads of cabbages were going in, and the hippies were sort of in and out of the two milieux, so it was a great place to be'.

Middle Earth.

But that changed when the police raided Middle Earth. Jenny Fabian says this happened because 'these strange people' had hired the place:

> One of the sort of the offshoots of the underground movement was you got these sort of cult movements who believed in cosmic rays and the Sun and the Earth being in alliance with each other and certain things had to happen, and they were celebrating some important moment and they all were chanting in a circle, and they had brought their children with them because there wasn't a drinks licence there, so it wasn't as though kids couldn't come in, and all this chanting and wailing obviously had sort of seeped through, and the market men up above, who come into the Covent Garden really early, don't they? – I'm not quite sure what time, but they obviously heard… they thought there was a child sacrifice going on. And so they called the police and they all came down and raided the place and wanted to arrest everybody for child sacrifice. That was quite frightening we all had to sort of run and try and squeeze out of a window the other end.

According to Jeff Dexter (who is quoted in Jonathon Green's book *Days in the Life: Voices from the English Underground, 1961–1971*), the police tipped off the Covent Garden porters, who proceeded to smash Middle Earth up while the police then took 70 minutes to answer the staff's distress call. Dexter says, 'That was the death of Middle Earth, really.'

## The Arts Lab
## No. 182 Drury Lane
## London, WC2B 5PP

The Arts Lab was set up in July 1967 by Jim Haynes, an American who had previously co-founded the Traverse Theatre in Edinburgh. It had a range of functions: a cinema (in the basement), a restaurant (on the first floor) run by (Barry) Miles' wife, Sue, a theatre (where Steven Berkoff put

The Arts Lab.

on his first production and where dancer Lindsay Kemp was a frequent performer), an art gallery (where John Lennon and Yoko Ono staged a sculpture exhibition) and a bookshop. David Bowie also used the Arts Lab for rehearsals.

If this all sounds too good to be true, then it probably was. The Arts Lab's open-door policy attracted large numbers of hangers-on. In *In the Sixties* (Barry) Miles says that viewers tended to remove their shoes before entering the cinema and so, even though the films were 'interesting' and the sexual tension 'palpable,' the smell of dirty feet was 'overwhelming.' In another memoir, *The Untold 60s*, Alex Gross, an American translator and theatre consultant who wrote for *IT*, says that towards the end Haynes started to employ Hells Angels on the door, in order to keep out the more 'unruly' elements. Gross says that the British Angels were a lot milder than their American counterparts and suggests that the Rolling Stones' inability to appreciate that led to the Altamont tragedy in December 1969 (the British contingent had provided security, without incident, at the Hyde Park concert that summer).

Haynes announced the Arts Lab's closure in a letter to 'Dear Friends' on Tuesday 28 October 1969. He told them that it had been 'a vision frustrated by an indifferent, fearful, and insecure society'. He then moved to Amsterdam, where he helped launch *Suck* – 'the magazine for sexual freedom'. He later taught Media Studies and Sexual Politics at the University of Paris.

## PROGRESS
### London, WC2H 7RJ

According to Stash de Rola, 'The first one of them all, back in '65, was the Ad Lib, and the Ad Lib had the merit of being upstairs, you know, clubs are usually in cellars, and it was absolutely amazing.' George Melly (in his book *Revolt into Style*) observed that its greatest asset was a huge window looking down on London. This, he argued, gave its clients (pop stars, fashion designers and young actors) the feeling of a conquered world.

The Ad Lib was on the top floor of a large building on the corner of Lisle Street. The club was above the Prince Charles Theatre, which has since become the Prince Charles cinema. Stash de

The Ad Lib Club.

Rola's view that it was 'the first one of them all' was shared by Jane Wilson, who called it the 'original discotheque' in her chapter 'Teenagers' in *Len Deighton's London Dossier* (1967). She then went on to explain that its popularity had waned, although the official reason for its closure (in late 1966) had been complaints about the noise. After the demise of the Ad Lib, Dolly's, the Scotch of St James and the Bag O'Nails vied for the title of 'London's hippest club'.

Nevertheless, the Ad Lib had a good run. It opened in December 1963, and this virtually coincided with the birth of Beatlemania (although George Melly believed that the club opened in February 1964). The Fab Four enjoyed going there, not least because people tended to leave them alone. Two famous Beatle events took place at the Ad Lib: Ringo Starr proposed to Maureen Cox (they tied the knot in February 1965), while John and Cynthia, George and Patti went there the fateful night when they first took LSD. This was after their coffee had been spiked during a dinner at the home of the devilish 'dentist to the stars,' John Riley. The red light in the Ad Lib's lift allegedly led the not-so-fabulous four to believe that it was on fire. Accounts vary as to the date of the episode. The authors of *The Beatles' London* say that it took place in July 1965, while in 2006 *Time Out* magazine claimed that it happened on Saturday 27 March.

In addition to the Beatles, other Ad Lib regulars included the Stones, the Kinks, Mary Quant, (dressmaker) Jean Muir, Hayley Mills, Julie Christie and Princess Margaret. Stash de Rola recalls: 'I remember being there with P.J. Proby and with Stuart Whitman the actor and it was such an incredible melting pot. Wonderful nights were spent at the Ad Lib.'

Today the site of the club is occupied by offices, although the fiery lift is said to be still in operation.

## Better Books
## No. 94 Charing Cross Road
## London, WC2H 0BP

Better Books was owned by Tony Godwin, who was also the editorial director of Penguin. He acquired the shop in the late 1940s. According to the standard version of events, it was just another bookshop until 1964, when Godwin went to San Francisco and visited Lawrence Ferlinghetti's City Lights bookstore, which was arguably the birthplace of the Beat Generation. The two began

Better Books.

exchanging books (City Lights for Penguin) and ideas, and a City Lights manager, Dick McBride, even moved to London to help 'bohemianise' Better Books.

It would appear, however, that another factor in the transformation of Better Books was the arrival of (Barry) Miles, who got a job there in January 1965. He was in touch with the Beats and, when Allen Ginsberg walked into the bookshop in the summer of 1965, he asked to speak to him. A reading at Better Books was quickly arranged. According to Miles (writing in *In the Sixties*) the audience included Donovan, Andy Warhol and the model Edie Sedgwick (who would die in 1971). Ginsberg's visit led to the International Poetry Incarnation at the Royal Albert Hall on 11 June.

The basement at Better Books was also the setting for some wild happenings, such as a 'fake disembowelling' in March 1965. They were organised by the sTigma group. Jeff Nuttall described these events in his 1968 book *Bomb Culture* (which was once considered a counter-cultural classic, but it is now out of print).

Miles left Better Books and helped set up Indica in October 1965. According to *Bomb Culture*, Better Books closed in 1967, around the same time as the UFO Club. It also got a mention in Piri Halasz's *A Swinger's Guide to London* (1967) as 'a hip place for trendy paperbacks and slightly shocking literature'.

## No. 212 Shaftesbury Avenue
## London, WC2H 8EB

Even if it probably didn't enjoy the same legendary status as No. 101 Cromwell Road, No. 212 Shaftesbury Avenue was a fun pad. For much of 1968 and '69 the turret at the top of it was, as one of its residents, Mick Farren, said, 'the classic band apartment' – in this case of his group, the Deviants. Farren, who described life there in *Give the Anarchist a Cigarette*, said that its proximity to the Arts Lab, Middle Earth and the IT offices meant that all sorts of interesting people dropped by, including 'Hells Angels from California'. He added that 'the rest of the tenants all seemed to be kind of visiting Swiss bankers, and, boy, did they not like us coming up and down in the lift!'

No. 212 was – and still is – part of the same building that contained the Shaftesbury Theatre. Farren recalled: 'The irony being that what was playing while we were living there was *Hair* so the tourists thought we were part of the company and we had an ongoing kind of grudge with the commissionaires because sometimes we'd mingle with the crowd and just wander in in the interval, and they didn't like that at all'.

No. 212 Shaftesbury Avenue.

Relations rapidly deteriorated: 'And I believe one of our demolition experts let off a naval distress flare during the second act because he was really pissed off with somebody who'd annoyed him. No, *Hair* didn't take kindly to the real thing invading it!'

The Deviants realised that they were about to be evicted from the turret and so 'we tossed the keys to the Hells Angels and they went in as squatters because the landlords had been rather unpleasant to us and so we had our revenge'.

## No. 22 Betterton Street
## London, WC2H 9BX

The *International Times* (*IT*) moved to this building from No. 102 Southampton Row in early 1968, as Mick Farren explained: 'Then Nigel Samuel, the mad 20-year-old millionaire, became involved and he bought a house, a building in Betterton Street in Covent Garden, and we moved in there for a while, and then Nigel went mad and I think Lord Goodman seized his assets because he was attempting to fund Michael X in a revolution in Trinidad, which didn't go down well with the British government!'

Farren said that *IT* then moved to nearby No. 27 Endell Street.

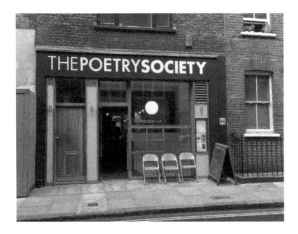

No. 22 Betterton Street.

# SW1

## The Indica Gallery
## No. 6 Mason's Yard
## London, *SW1Y* 6BU

It was here that Yoko Ono first met John Lennon. This momentous event probably took place on Monday 7 November 1966, when John attended a preview party two days before the opening of Yoko's first European exhibition, 'Unfinished Objects and Paintings'.

The gallery, which takes its name from the botanical term *cannabis indica* was the brainchild of MAD Ltd, a triumvirate consisting of (Barry) Miles; Jane's brother, (Peter) Asher; and Marianne Faithfull's then husband, (John) Dunbar. They chose No. 6 Mason's Yard on account of its proximity to the trendy Scotch of St James Club at No. 13. Originally, Indica was both a bookshop and gallery, and it opened in March 1966. Paul McCartney designed the wrapping paper and helped put up the shelves, in addition to investing £5,000. That summer, some months before John and Yoko's historic encounter, the bookshop part moved to No. 102 Southampton Row, which also became the office of the *International Times*.

The Indica Gallery.

In his memoir, *In the Sixties*, Miles tells us that 'John Lennon arrived in his chauffeur-driven Mini Cooper'. He had been invited by John Dunbar, who introduced him to Yoko. She claimed not to know who the Beatles were, although, Miles reveals, she had been to meet Paul McCartney the previous week. Yoko continues to maintain her innocence to this day. According to a profile by the historian Simon Schama ('Give Yoko a Chance' in *The Financial Times*, 2 June 2012), 'She insists she really had no idea who he was or what he did.' Not only that, Yoko manages to persuade Schama to take the somewhat unorthodox view that she would have achieved international fame even if she hadn't met John Lennon.

Robin Williamson, formerly of the Incredible String Band, also has a positive take on Yoko. He recalls going to have tea with her before she met John. She was, he says, 'A wonderful artist, with a house full of extraordinary pieces of art, like sheets of glass hung by threads from the ceiling and little paintings that you could only see if you climbed up on the ladder and looked at them with a magnifying glass at the top of the ladder; that sort of thing. Conceptual paintings and conceptual pieces of art. Yeah, I think she was brilliant.'

Nor does he subscribe to the 'Yoko as Lady Macbeth' school:

> I think people wrong her, probably. I mean, women's position in the world of music in the '60s was precarious, to say the least, and it was a heavily male-dominated era, and it had been for a long time. Things have changed slightly, but I think women are still under-acknowledged, or less so than they were then. And I think Yoko came in for a lot of flak that she didn't deserve. So did Linda McCartney.

John Lennon was similarly impressed by Yoko's *Blue Room Event* piece, which also required climbing a ladder to look through a magnifying glass, hanging from the ceiling, in order to read the word 'Yes'. Miles says the show was a success. Roman Polanski and his then girlfriend Sharon Tate (who was murdered by the followers of Charles Manson in Los Angeles in August 1969) went to see it on several occasions.

# The Scotch of St James
# No. 13 Mason's Yard
# London, SW1 6BU

According to Stash de Rola:

> The Scotch of St James was, at one point in '66, the general hang-out of all the musicians in London, practically, and one, nightly, would meet up with the likes of Jonathan King, who had that hit with 'Everyone's Gone to the Moon', and Eric Burdon was there and nearly everyone from The Who too, you name it. I mean, it was a place where one jammed, where one spent a lot of time.

The Scotch of St James opened for business on Tuesday 30 March 1965. Later that year George Melly wrote a piece about London 'hippy joints', which he later reproduced in his 1970 book *Revolt into Style*. He interviewed the club's manager, Rod Harrod, who had previously worked at the Cromwellian. Harrod didn't deny that he had once thrown out a customer for asking George Harrison for his autograph and he boasted that he had once turned away a party of American millionaires who wanted to sit at a table reserved for Mick Jagger and Chrissie Simpson, thereby losing an estimated £50 in business. He told Melly that the Beatles and the Stones were never made to pay, nor were members of Eric Burdon's group, the Animals. This was for their loyalty in following Harrod from

The Scotch of St James.

the Cromwellian. At the end of the interview Harrod took a phone call from Kensington Palace and proudly announced that Princess Margaret and Lord Snowdon would be arriving in five minutes.

And yet the following year *The New London Spy* complained that it had become too loud for 'whispering sweet nothings into a lady's ear,' while in 1967 *Len Deighton's London Dossier* claimed that 'the Scotch' had replaced the Ad Lib, before being succeeded 'very briefly' by the Cromwellian, although as of 1967 Dolly's was 'the place to go'. Piri Halasz (1967) said that it was friendlier and more intimate than Dolly's. Dallas and Fantoni tell us that the menu included steak and salad for 15s, and that breakfast was free. Although the Beatles were regular guests and even had their own table, Stash de Rola, who would later befriend them, used to go to the Scotch with another Liverpudlian musician:

> A constant companion in those days was John Banks, who was the drummer of the Merseybeats, and he was very funny because he was obsessed … he was an obsessive pill popper and he'd ask anybody, regardless who it was, he'd say, 'Have you got any pills?' sometimes to the utter consternation of a journalist or something, any pills would do, you know, upper or downers!

Banks's penchant for pills could explain why he died at the age of forty-four in 1988. And if *Len Deighton's London Dossier* claimed that the Cromwellian and Dolly's overtook the Scotch, then Stash de Rola names another club: '[The Scotch] was a great hangout, a bit like the Speakeasy would become later on. You know, a year later the Speakeasy had taken over.'

# Dalmeny Court
# No. 8 Duke Street
# London, SW1Y 6BL

This apartment building, which was a stone's throw from the Indica Gallery and the Scotch of St James, had some distinguished residents in the 1960s. According to (Barry) Miles' book, *London Calling*, they included Animals lead singer Eric Burdon, *Naked Lunch* author William Burroughs,

Dalmeny Court.

and two of Burroughs's friends, 'sound poet' Brian Gysin ('the only man I ever respected,' according to Burroughs) and film director Antony Balch.

The building's proximity to the Scotch of St James was handy for Burdon, who was a regular. He is generally thought to have been the inspiration for the Eggman in 'I am the Walrus'. Burdon was known as 'Eggs' to his friends, on account of his alleged for breaking eggs over the bodies of naked women.

# The Economist Plaza
# St James's Street
# London, SW1A 1HG

The Economist Plaza and its buildings feature in two Swinging London movies, namely Michelangelo Antonioni's *Blow-Up* (1966) and Michael Winner's less well known *I'll Never Forget What's'isname* (1967). In *Blow-Up* it is the setting for the opening sequence in which 'rag week' students dressed as mime artists run riot in a Land Rover. *I'll Never Forget What'sisname*, on the other hand, begins with disgruntled advertising executive Andrew Quint (played by Oliver Reed) marching into work one morning carrying an axe. Once inside the headquarters of the Lute Organisation (the Economist Building), he proceeds to hack his desk to pieces. This is because he wants to quit both his job and his marriage, and he spends the rest of the film trying to get away from his wife, Louise (Wendy Craig, who also began acting in the famous TV comedy *Not in Front of the Children* that year) and his boss, Jonathan Lute (Orson Welles). During the course of the film we witness Andrew's relationships with a series of beautiful women: Georgina (Carol White), Josie (Marianne Faithfull) and Susannah (Lyn Ashley, who would later marry Monty Python's Eric Idle). As Andrew endeavours to woo Georgina he takes her in his sports car to an old boys' reunion at his public school, where we meet his former headmaster (Michael Hordern), and later to Cambridge to visit his former tutor (Harry Andrews). Edward Fox is also in the cast of an interesting film that contains some surreal, dream-like sequences. The movie was also one of the first to feature the f-word: for the record, it was uttered by Marianne Faithfull.

The Economist Plaza.

The Economist Plaza was designed by the husband and wife team of Alison and Peter Smithson and completed in 1964. Even today its new brutalist modernity contrasts with the elegant eighteenth-century buildings that surround it. It's easy to see why film directors were attracted to the plaza in the 1960s. The Economist Building received Grade II listing in 1988.

## The Crazy Elephant/Dolly's
## No. 57 Jermyn Street
## London, SW1

Dolly's appears in Piri Halasz's seminal 1966 Swinging London article for *Time* magazine, in which we discover (in 'SCENE FOUR') that Jane Ormsby-Gore (twenty-three) goes dancing there with her boyfriend, Hung On You owner Michael Rainey (twenty-five) after having attended an opening at Robert's Fraser's gallery. Later in the article Halasz calls it one of London's three 'reigning' discotheques. The other two are its 'rival' – The Scotch of St James – and Annabel's.

Dolly's previous incarnation, the Crazy Elephant, had been the setting for an unfortunate episode involving the actor Oliver Reed (1938–99). As he later admitted in his autobiography, *Reed All About Me* (1979), he went there one night in 1964, after having completed work on the film, *The System*. A group of young toughs sitting at a table called him 'a vampire' (a reference to his horror films) and, when he answered back, they smashed a glass in his face, threw him to the ground, and kicked him repeatedly. The facial scars were so bad that Reed briefly quit acting and started selling shop signs.

The Crazy Elephant was, however, to prove to be a more positive place for another star of the 1960s. Brian Auger remembers an encounter early in 1965:

> One night a guy comes up to me, and says, 'I've got this great singer,' and I went, 'Oh, really?' And he says 'Yeah, he'd love to sit in with you.' And I said, 'Well, like, why don't you bring him up during the break, and we'll take a look at him, and I'll have a talk to him.' The guy comes up, a very nice guy, really great, with a heavy Welsh accent. And I said, 'So, how long have you been in

London, then?' he says, 'Oh, two years,' he says, 'I've just made this single, and if it doesn't go, I'm going back to Wales, actually, 'because I can make a decent living in the miners' clubs'. So I said, 'Oh, OK. So, what's your name, by the way?' He says, 'Tom Jones.'

Auger continues:

I said, 'Yeah, OK, mate, what do you want to sing?' And he says, 'Do you know, like Lucille?' I said, 'Sure, sure.' So we start the riff for Lucille and we give him the microphone, and this guy starts to sing, and we're all like, 'Wow!' Afterwards he sang a couple of things with us, and I wished him good luck, and he said, 'Thanks, boyo.' And he's like really cool and two weeks later: Bang! 'It's Not Unusual'!

Auger also remembers that the club 'was downstairs, you had to load the organ down the stairs and everything, but Paul and Ringo used to come and they'd be sitting in the audience, you know, they'd have a drink, hang out, whatever, and that kind of happened several times'.

The change from the Crazy Elephant to Dolly's probably took place in early 1966. As Piri Halasz states in her 1967 book, *A Swinger's Guide to London*, the name Dolly's was based on the successful musical *Hello Dolly*, which opened in the West End in December 1965.

In actual fact, Halasz suggests that by 1967 Dolly's and the Scotch of St James had become 'a trifle passé,' but she says that they were still sufficiently prestigious to charge 3 guineas for temporary membership. Halasz's view that Dolly's had started to fade by 1967, wasn't shared by Jane Wilson in *Len Deighton's London Dossier*. For her Dolly's was still 'the place to go – but it may not be by next week.' She describes it as 'a long dark room with coats at one end and loos at the other,' yet she says that you can see Mick Jagger's white trousers 'gleaming through the gloom'.

The Crazy Elephant/Dolly's.

## No. 29 Lennox Gardens
## London, SW1X ODE

Marianne Faithfull and her husband John Dunbar lived in an apartment here with their son Nicholas, who was born in November 1965. Marianne Faithfull left in 1967 when she moved in with Mick Jagger at Harley House. Life in Lennox Gardens is chronicled in her 1994 autobiography *Faithfull*. Although her own drug habit has been well documented, in the book we learn that John Dunbar, a Cambridge-educated poet, liked to put liquid methedrine in his coffee of a morning before going off to work at Indica. Marianne Faithfull explains that 'American junkies' often stayed at Lennox Gardens and that the reason they came to London was not the vibrant cultural scene so much as the fact that 'British pharmaceutical heroin' could still be obtained legally. She describes No. 29 Lennox Gardens as a junkies' crash pad, while admitting that she herself was spending increasing amounts of time with Brian Jones, Anita Pallenberg and Keith Richards at No. 1 Courtfield Road. The raising of Nicholas was largely left to a nanny, something Stash de Rola confirms: 'I'd met Paul McCartney, I suppose, in '66 at Marianne Faithfull's house. He was dating Marianne Faithfull's nanny. Marianne Faithfull had a son called Nicholas Dunbar, and Nicholas had a nanny called Maggie and she was very cute and Paul McCartney was dating her at one point, more or less secretly.'

No. 29 Lennox Gardens.

# SW3

## La Bottega di San Lorenzo
## Nos 21–25 Beauchamp Place
## London, SW3 1NH

According to the staff at this Italian restaurant in Beauchamp Place, it opened for business in October 1963 – the same month that Beatlemania officially took off, and one month before the assassination of President Kennedy.

Piri Halasz (1967) describes the decor as being in 'a simple Italian peasant style,' and, more importantly perhaps, she tells us that director Michelangelo Antonioni regularly ate there when he was making the cult movie *Blow-Up* (which was released in 1966).

Dallas and Fantoni and *Len Deighton's London Dossier* (1967) refer to it as the 'Osteria San Lorenzo'. Dallas and Fantoni tell us that the owner's name was Lorenzo Berne, while the *Dossier* informs us that it was 'remarkably inexpensive' and 'so crowded that you should book well in advance'.

La Bottega di San Lorenzo.

Bazaar
(Brompton Road).

## Bazaar

## No. 46 Brompton Road

## London, SW3 1BW

Even though the original building has been demolished, this was the location of Mary Quant's second Bazaar store. It opened in 1957 and its interior was designed by Terence Conran. According to Dallas and Fantoni (1967) its hours were 9.30 to 6 p.m., although it closed at 1 p.m. on Saturdays, presumably in recognition of the fact that young clothes shoppers would gravitate towards the King's Road of a Saturday afternoon.

## No. 3 Cheyne Walk

## London, SW3 5QZ

Keith Richards bought this impressive 'town house' in May 1968 but, as he relates in *Life* (2010), he didn't particularly enjoy his time there. This was because the police, who weren't satisfied with the results of the Redlands bust at his Sussex home in 1967, were still on his case. He would often come back to Cheyne Walk in the small hours of the morning and be greeted by members of the drug squad who would leap out of the bushes, truncheons at the ready.

    *Life* also details Richards's drug-related activities at Cheyne Walk. It was here that he and his friend and fellow musician Gram Parsons (who would die of an overdose at the Joshua Tree Inn in the California desert in 1973) unsuccessfully tried a cold turkey technique that had been recommended by William Burroughs. Richards explains that police harassment, combined with the high level of income tax, prompted the Stones to move to France in the summer of 1971. Richards sold the property in 1978.

No. 3 Cheyne Walk.

## No. 48 Cheyne Walk
## London, SW3 5LP

Mick Jagger bought this house for £50,000 in May 1968, the same month that Keith Richards bought No. 3. But, as his former girlfriend Marianne Faithfull relates in her 1994 autobiography *Faithfull*, life there was far from idyllic. She didn't like the constant parade of guests and hangers-on,

No. 48 Cheyne Walk.

and she says that her relationship with Jagger had now become largely platonic. As a result, they both had numerous affairs, with members of both sexes. She admits that her first affair at Cheyne Walk was with Stash de Rola, who allegedly scaled the wisteria to reach the first-floor balcony when Mick Jagger was out at an all-night session at a recording studio. This Romeo and Juliet-like gesture prompted the memorable comment, 'Well, that deserves a fuck!' The current authors tried to get Stash de Rola to reminisce about Cheyne Walk, but, ever the gentlemen, he steered the conversation towards Christopher Gibbs's place at No. 100.

In *Faithfull* Marianne describes how her mental health went into decline while living at No. 48 Cheyne Walk. She was badly affected by the death of Brian Jones in July 1969 and shortly after that she overdosed while in Sydney with Mick Jagger. Yet in January 2013 she told *The Daily Mail* that the real negative turning point in her life had probably been the Redlands bust in February 1967. She moved out of Cheyne Walk in 1970 and, she says, started living in an alley in Soho soon afterwards. Jagger sold the house in 1978, the same year that Richards sold No. 3.

## No. 5 Cheltenham Terrace
## London, SW3 4RD

'Whatever Happened to P. J. Proby?' asked Van Morrison in 2002. Proby had been a big name in the 1960s, as Nigel Lesmoir-Gordon recalled:

> P. J. Proby had an amazing house in Chelsea. I remember going there one night, tripping with him, and Donovan was there, and Donovan was crying on the stairs, he was very, very upset. And I felt a bit out of it and I was standing at one end of the room and I remember P.J. Proby going, 'Come over here, Lone Ranger!'

The house was the subject of a brief TV report by another important '60s figure who subsequently disappeared from the limelight – Simon Dee. Dee went to interview Proby at his home. P. J. Proby

No. 5 Cheltenham Terrace.

(real name James Marcus Smith) was born in Houston, Texas, in 1938 and moved to England in 1964. That year he enjoyed hits like 'Hold Me' and 'Somewhere', but his career began to stall at the end of the decade. He was tried (and acquitted) at Worcester Crown Court for benefit fraud in 2012. Simon Dee (real name Cyril Nicholas Henty-Dodd) died of cancer in 2009.

## Guys 'N' Dolls
## No. 74 King's Road
## London, SW3 4TZ

Guys 'N' Dolls was mentioned in Piri Halasz's 1966 article for *Time* magazine. In 'SCENE TWO' Mick Jagger stops in at the coffee house with *Ready, Steady, Go!* presenter Cathy McGowan. Jagger sees a young girl reading French *Vogue* and informs her, 'Luv, you've got it upside down.'

The following year Guys 'N' Dolls appeared in an iconic photograph showing three bikini-clad models drinking from bottles of Coke at a table on the pavement as bewildered and not particularly hip members of the public look on. In 1967 it was listed in the 'Food' chapter of *Len Deighton's London Dossier* as a place where you could eat at any time of the day. It was open 24 hours a day, although breakfast was served from '10 a.m. right up until it becomes lunch'.

It's known that Kenny Everett, then a DJ with Radio London, went there around 1965. He lived nearby at Bristol House on Lower Sloane Street.

Guys 'N' Dolls.

The Chelsea Drugstore.

## The Chelsea Drugstore
## No. 49 King's Road
## London, SW3 4ND

'I went down to the Chelsea drugstore, To get your prescription filled.' So sings Mick Jagger in the Rolling Stones song 'You Can't Always Get What You Want', which was recorded in November 1968. The Chelsea Drugstore, which featured a chrome and glass renovation of a more traditional building, opened earlier that year. It stood on the corner of King's Road and Royal Avenue. You can still admire the futuristic architecture today, even though the building is now occupied by a McDonald's.

The Chelsea Drugstore was also used as a location in Stanley Kubrick's 1971 film adaptation of Anthony Burgess' 1962 novel *A Clockwork Orange*. It appears as a record store where Alex (Malcolm McDowell) picks up a couple of young girls.

## Club dell'Aretusa
## No. 107 King's Road
## London, SW3 4PA

Quiz question: What do the Beatles and the Kray twins have in common? Answer: They ate at the Club dell'Aretusa, as did Twiggy, Michael Caine, Terence Stamp and Richard Harris, not to mention Peter Sarstedt, who wrote and sang the 1969 international hit 'Where Do You Go To (My Lovely)?'.

The club and restaurant, which opened in 1967, was set up by Alvaro Maccioni with the idea of building on the success of Alvaro's; although, as Alasdair Scott Sutherland points out in *The Spaghetti Tree*, it ended up eclipsing it.

Club dell'Aretusa.

Scott Sutherland says that it became the place to go for Saturday lunch and he recalls seeing Sammy Davis Jr there:

> So he arrives, walks up the stairs onto the open terrace, which is already full of people dressed in their finest, going out to lunch on Saturday, and he climbs up on a table and starts singing 'O Sole Mio' at Alvaro. But somebody outside in the street saw him standing on a chair singing from across the road in the King's Road because this was a terrace. And suddenly there was a crowd of five, six hundred people all stopping the traffic on the King's Road, photographers snapping, and of course Sammy Davis goes to the edge of the building and starts waving as if he was giving a royal performance. Then you wonder, you look back at the cuttings and the stories saying that London was the centre of the world.

# The Chelsea Potter
# 119 Kings Road
# Chelsea SW3 4PL

The Chelsea Potter was a very cool watering hole in the 1960s, being the favourite pub of many a rock star, writer and artist. It appears in at least two stories about that decade. One concerns the playwright Joe Orton who, it is alleged, met a friend, Peter Nolan, here on Saturday 5 August 1967. Orton was unhappy about his relationship with Kenneth Halliwell, with whom he shared a small flat at No. 25 Noel Road in Islington. He confided to Nolan that he had found a new boyfriend and that he wanted to end his relationship with Halliwell, but didn't know how to go about it. Four days later Orton found the courage to tell Halliwell, who reacted by killing him and then himself.

In 1968 Los Angeleno Jim Morrison (lead singer of the Doors and self-styled poet maudit) became a regular at the Chelsea Potter. According to one account, he would 'prop up the bar, searching for 'Swinging London'." Morrison also went to an early grave, overdosing in Paris in 1971, at the age of twenty-seven.

Morrison, who enjoyed his drink, may have been attracted by the Chelsea Potter's impressive selection. According to Adrian Bailey's chapter on 'Drink' in *Len Deighton's London Dossier*

The Chelsea Potter.

(1967): 'The landlord claims to have the largest variety of aperitifs and spirits in London, including such exotica as tequila and saké, and keeps forty different wines to serve by the glass.'

Dallas and Fantoni (1967) tell us that the landlord's name was John Bishop. We also learn that it was 'an old London pub now patronised by the Chelsea set who can be observed through the plain glass windows'.

## Hung on You (1)
## No. 22 Cale Street
## London, SW3 3QU

This was the original location of Hung on You, which was without doubt one of Chelsea's – and indeed London's – groovier boutiques. The store was run by Michael Rainey and his wife Jane Ormsby-Gore, who was the daughter of the 5th Baron Harlech (1918–85), a one-time Conservative MP and ambassador to the United States. Michael Rainey and Jane Ormsby-Gore both feature in Piri Halasz's Swinging London article in *Time* magazine (15 April 1966).

Michael Rainey opened Hung On You in late 1965, taking the name from a song released by the Righteous Brothers (and written by Gerry Goffin, Carole King and Phil Spector) earlier that year. The store rapidly attracted clients such as the Beatles, the Who and the Rolling Stones. It was more 'psychedelic' and Victorian than other boutiques at that time: in an oft-quoted comment by Nik Cohn, 'When you shopped at Hung On You, you felt like both Oscar Wilde and Captain Marvel, locked up inside one body.' In an interview at the V&A in 2006 Jane Ormsby-Gore modestly stated: 'My contribution to Hung on You was purely talking and discussing things at home,' but, she added, 'we were very influenced by Byron ... those Byron shirts with frilly fronts and big sleeves. And literature: Spencer's Fairie Queene ... that sort of mood, rather romantic. He [Michael Rainey – ed.] would find ... lovely materials, all made in London in the East End by proper old-fashioned tailors'.

*The New London Spy* (1966) gives the address as '22 Cate Street [*sic*]', while telling us that 'Michael Rainey or Christopher Lynch will design you a suit in olive velveteen or forties stripes which will be made up in ten days. Also more conventional materials. Mick Jagger and others

Hung on You,
No. 22 Cale Street.

buy their suits from 35 gns., jackets from 20 gns., trousers from 8 gns.' Halasz (1967) describes it as a 'tremendously "in" shop,' while Dallas and Fantoni (1967) give the hours of business (10 a.m. to 7 p.m.).

Hung On You moved to No. 430 King's Road in late 1967. Later No. 22 Cale Street had something of a '60s revival when Paul McCartney's former girlfriend opened the 'Jane Asher Party Cakes and Sugarcraft Shop' but the premises were subsequently taken over by a branch of Paxton & Whitfield, 'Britain's leading cheesemonger'.

## Alvaro's
## No. 124 King's Road
## London, SW3 4TR

> We all flocked along to the opening party. Within four days it was full. I mean, the opening party spilled out into the street and the police were called and they had to disperse the crowds to let the traffic down the King's Road. And suddenly the emphasis of where the most cool place in London was for us – I was 20 – moved from Soho to the King's Road.

Alasdair Scott Sutherland was present at the opening of Alvaro's on April Fool's Day in 1966. He adds:

> And I was there four nights later, and in came a party of four, including Princess Margaret, and about an hour-and-a-half later, after having done his show in the West End, in came Sammy Davis with three other people. And, from what I understand from Alvaro, Princess Margaret said, 'Oh, I'd love to meet Sammy Davis!' So Alvaro goes over and fetches him and, of course Alvaro has been working in the Terrazza for five years, he already knows Princess Margaret, so he knows what to say, so he brings over Sammy Davis Jr, he says, 'Your Royal Highness, may I have the honour to present Mr Sammy Davis Jr?' And there's lots of bowing and excitement and Sammy Davis sits down and spends 10 minutes talking to Princess Margaret. Apparently, she'd already booked tickets to see his show.

Alvaro's.

This story gives credence to the comment attributed to the magazine *London Life*: 'The name Alvaro's is whispered from the studios of show biz to the courts of Royalty.' The restaurant was the creation of Alvaro Maccioni, who had quit his job as manager at the fashionable 'Tratt' (Trattoria La Terrazza) in Soho. His former bosses, Mario Cassandro and Franco Lagattolla, naturally felt betrayed when they realised that he had also poached several of the waiters, much of the menu, and numerous clients. The list was certainly impressive. Halasz (1967) says that Len Deighton, Leslie Caron, Michael Caine and 'The Shrimp' (Jean Shrimpton) 'gave the place their blessing when it opened,' while Sutherland's book *The Spaghetti Tree* also mentions Twiggy and her husband Justin de Villeneuve, as well as Sean Connery. It was also fairly close to the home of Brian Jones and Anita Pallenberg in Courtfield Road, and they went there most evenings with Marianne Faithfull, according to the latter's autobiography, *Faithfull*.

Halasz tells us the waiters wore T-shirts and that the place attracted some of London's most beautiful women, particularly at lunch, when Alvaro offered ladies a discount. Dallas and Fantoni (1967) simply list the hours: 12.30 to 3 p.m. and 7 p.m. to 11.30 p.m., while *Len Deighton's London Dossier* (1967) gives only the telephone number (KEN 6296), which was technically ex-directory.

Alvaro Maccioni also opened the Club dell'Aretusa on the King's Road, but sold up and returned to Italy in 1972. He came back to London in 1975 and opened a restaurant in World's End, La Famiglia.

# Quorum
# No. 52 Radnor Walk
# London, SW3 4BN

Quorum, in spite of being located in a terraced house in a residential street, was frequented by the Beatles and the Stones. It was run by Alice Pollock, who employed the services of fashion designer Ossie Clark and textile designer Celia Birtwell. They were later immortalised, along with their cat, by David Hockney, in his 1971 painting, *Mr. and Mrs. Clark and Percy*, which hangs in the Tate Gallery. Another artist, Duggie Fields (1945–2021), remembers that Alice Pollock had originally set

Quorum.

up shop in Kensington: 'For a while Alice had the most trendy fashion shop in London. She took on Ossie Clark out of college and they used to design both together and separately. When they moved to Radnor Walk the Models One agency started off as English Boy in an office above, and Brian Jones also lived in the same building, so it was very much a sort of social scene.'

And, as Fields said, Alice Pollock had an unusual approach to retail:

> You never knew who you were going to meet at Quorum, but Alice, on a Saturday, for some reason, would frequently lock the door of the shop, and people would turn up and she'd go up to the door and just go, 'Fuck off! Fuck off!' If she didn't know them or she didn't like them. If she liked them, then they got invited in, and 'in' was sort of like a very small, select, glamorous party with joints and sometimes champagne.

Alice Pollock is also listed as one of the twenty-four 'People Who Make London Swing' by Dallas and Fantoni (1967). We learn that the then twenty-four-year-old shopowner was born in Southern Rhodesia, drank vodka and tonic and smoked Consulate. The book also lists Quorum in its 'Female Fashion' section, telling us that it was officially open from Monday from Saturday from 10 a.m. to 6 p.m., and that its underwear cost anything from £1 to £3, while its clothes ranged from £3 to £30.

Given Duggie Fields's comments, it isn't entirely surprising that Quorum ran up debts. It was bought by retailer Alfred Radley, who also sponsored Ossie Clark's individual dress collections. At the time Clark employed a young driver called David Gilmour, who left at the start of 1968 in order to replace Syd Barrett in Pink Floyd.

Ossie Clark and Celia Birtwell divorced in 1974 and Ossie later went bankrupt. He was killed by a male lover on 6 August 1996.

# Picasso Restaurant
# No. 127 King's Road
# London, SW3 4PW

This small establishment (which was Italian, in spite of the Spanish name) had a very interesting clientele in the 1960s. According to one account, Michael Caine and his mate Terence Stamp would 'hang out' there and 'pick up birds'. It is also said that when Italian director Michelangelo Antonioni

The Picasso Restaurant.

was shooting scenes in the neighbourhood for his quintessential Swinging London movie *Blow-Up* (1966), lead actor David Hemmings would come here and fortify himself with shots of vodka. Eric Clapton, another man who was fond of his drink, was a regular, as were the Rolling Stones, some of whose members were similarly prone to substance abuse.

# 4 Chelsea Manor Studios
# Nos 1–11 Flood Street
# London SW3 5SR

This was the studio of photographer Michael Cooper, and the Beatles gathered here on the evening of Thursday 30 March 1967. This was in order to work on one of the most famous album covers of all time: *Sgt. Pepper's Lonely Hearts Club Band*. It was the creation of Peter Blake and his then wife Jann Howorth, while the 'art direction' was by the notoriously miserly gallery owner Robert Fraser. Several decades later, Blake still resented the fact that he only received £200 for his efforts. He was also unhappy about being associated primarily with *Sgt. Pepper*, at the expense of his other work.

As (Barry) Miles recounts in his memoir *In the Sixties*, that evening Fraser was being 'immensely important,' even though he didn't really have anything to do, while Michael Cooper's toddler, Adam, crawled around the set. Miles adds that most people present were amused when the Beatles appeared in their colourful military uniforms, although the Fabulous Four failed to see the joke.

Nor was the *Sgt. Pepper* cover shoot the only interesting thing that happened in Flood Street that year. Denis and Margaret Thatcher and their teenage twins Carol and Mark moved in across the road at No. 19, which they are believed to have acquired for £28,000. They sold it in 1986, the same year that Robert Fraser died of AIDS-related illness. Michael Cooper died of a heroin overdose in 1973. Both men had been present at the police raid on Keith Richards' Redlands home in Sussex a few weeks before the *Sgt. Pepper* shoot. It is said that the inclusion of a doll in a 'Welcome Rolling Stones' sweater on the cover was a declaration of solidarity for Mick and Keith.

Michael Cooper's studio was on the ground floor, at the back of the building.

Chelsea Manor Studios.

# Bazaar/Alexander's
# No. 138a King's Road
# London, SW3 4XB

Halasz (1967) describes this as the 'grandmamma of them all' in terms of 'the mod boutique.' It was opened in 1955 by future miniskirt inventor Mary Quant and her partner Alexander Plunket-Greene ('APG'), whom she had met at Goldsmiths College. Their venture was helped by the fact that Plunket-Greene inherited £5,000 on his twenty-first birthday. The third partner in the business was an older entrepreneur, Archie McNair, who invested £8,000.

The ground floor was taken up by Bazaar while a restaurant, Alexander's, occupied the basement. This was later sold to the staff, but it kept its name. The success of Quant was such that a second branch opened at 46 Brompton Road in 1957. All three establishments thrived in the 1960s as Mary Quant (who received an OBE in 1966) evolved into a global brand. According to *The Guardian* (in a 2000 article by Audrey Gillan about Ms. Quant being bought out by her Japanese partners), 'By 1969 it was estimated up to 7 million women had a Quant label in their wardrobe.'

Bazaar/Alexander's, King's Road.

# The Pheasantry
# No. 152 King's Road
# London, SW3 4UT

According to (Barry) Miles, 'That's where Germaine Greer lived, Mickey Farren lived there. Eric Clapton lived there, Martin Sharp, the Australian psychedelic poster artist. I mean it wasn't exactly the Chelsea Hotel, but it was an important scene, you could go there and have fun. There was always somebody you knew.'

Mick Farren didn't live at the Pheasantry, but, as he explained in *Give the Anarchist a Cigarette*, he was a frequent guest of Germaine Greer, with whom he had 'a brief but memorable affair' in 1969. The couple enjoyed large amounts of 'conversation and sex,' and he even recalled her painting her new flat 'at the fashionable Pheasantry' without any clothes on (for practical purposes, apparently). It was during her time at the Pheasantry that Germaine Greer wrote her famous feminist manifesto, *The Female Eunuch*, which was published in 1970.

Greer's fellow Australian Martin Sharp enjoyed a fruitful working relationship with his neighbour at the Pheasantry, Eric Clapton, providing the lyrics for the Cream song 'Tales of Brave Ulysses' and the graphic design for two albums covers, *Disraeli Gears* (1967 – 'Tales of Brave Ulysses' was one of the tracks) and *Wheels of Fear* (1968).

Clapton's experience at the Pheasantry was marred by a visit from the notorious drug squad detective Sgt Norman Pilcher, who announced his arrival with his calling cry, 'Postman, special delivery!' Clapton, the story goes, managed to escape from the back of the building.

The Pheasantry, like Eric Clapton, went through a rough patch in the 1970s, and there were plans for its demolition. It was, however, saved thanks to the efforts of, among others, the poet John Betjeman – another distinguished Chelsea resident.

*Above left and right*: The Pheasantry.

## Dandie Fashions Tailoring for Men/Apple Tailoring (Civil and Theatrical)

## No. 161 King's Road

## London, SW3 5XP

This was the location of the boutique Dandie Fashions, which later became the short-lived, Beatle-owned Apple Tailoring (Civil and Theatrical).

Dandie Fashions was run by, among others, Australian John Crittle, who has been described as a 'sorely underrated figure' in the story of Swinging London. Crittle got a job at Michael Rainey's Hung on You, but the two men didn't get on. It has been said that Rainey, an aspiring aristocrat who was married to Jane Ormsby-Gore, tended to look down on Crittle, a 'Larrikin in London'. They agreed to go their separate ways and Crittle set up his own store, Dandie Fashions. His partners and investors in the new venture included another aristocrat, Guinness heir Tara Browne (who ran a tailoring business, Foster & Tara), Neil Winterbotham (who was also involved in the Middle Earth club in Covent Garden) and Freddie Hornik (who later acquired Granny Takes a Trip). Eighteen-year-old Alan Holston was hired to become manager.

Dandie Fashion's original premises were at No. 56 Queens Gate Mews and, according to *The Gear Guide* (1967), when the shop opened 'the Rolling Stones bought the entire stock'. The book also claimed that it moved to No. 161 King's Road in February that year. Tara Browne was killed in car crash on 18 December 1966, an event that partially inspired the *Sgt. Pepper* song 'A Day in the Life'. At this point Crittle acquired Browne's share in the business.

The King's Road location attracted the likes of Jimi Hendrix (who bought at least two floral jackets, and even slept there), Brian Jones and a not-yet-famous David Bowie. It also attracted the attention of the police, who made a drugs bust, arresting Crittle in May 1967. Brian Jones provided a chauffeur to take Crittle to his court appearance.

Paul McCartney picked up a Chinese-style yellow silk Mandarin jacket at Dandie, while John Lennon was also pally with Crittle. This could explain why Apple, which opened a boutique in Baker Street in December 1967, decided to invest in the business. Apple acquired 50 per cent of

Dandie Fashions/Apple Tailoring.

Dandie in February 1968. A launch party was held on Wednesday 22 May and Apple Tailoring opened to the public the following day. Crittle was no longer a shareholder, but he stayed on as director. The building's basement became the premises of Apple hairdressing, which was run by the Beatles' barber of choice, Leslie Cavendish.

The idea behind Apple Tailoring was to provide a more upmarket service than that available at Baker Street, but, like many Apple ventures, it proved to be a disaster. It only lasted a few months and Apple effectively gave the business back to Crittle.

Crittle later moved back to Australia. He left a young family behind him, one of whose members grew up to become Darcey Bussell, a ballerina and *Strictly Come Dancing* judge. John Crittle died in 2000.

## Chelsea Antique Market
## No. 253 King's Road
## London, SW3 5EL

According to Halasz (1967), the Chelsea Antique Market opened for business in September 1965. It was a great hit with the flower children, as Brian Auger, who played alongside Julie Driscoll in groups like Trinity and Steampacket (which also included Rod Stewart), recalls:

> And then we found the Chelsea Antique Market, where they sold all these old clothes and, of course, Julie Driscoll looked phenomenal in that stuff, and I used to dress out of there with Edwardian jackets and I looked like Lord Byron, or somebody! And the strange thing is you could walk out in the street, with all this stuff on and nobody batted an eyelid in England, I mean it was just like, 'Oh, well, you know...' It was great!

Halasz lists the address as No. 253 King's Road and describes the typical items on sale ('Victorian sewing machines, 1920's Charleston dresses and Tibetan praying sticks'), adding that the place is 'not cheap but colorful,' and that it has a 'snack bar and patio for watching the Saturday King's Road promenade'.

According to the 1966 street directory, 253 was still officially the premises of 'Harold Hill (Decorators) Ltd.' The antique market later moved to nearby Sydney Street.

Chelsea Antique Market.

# Le Reve
# No. 330 Kings Road
# London, SW3 5UR

Le Reve was clearly a very cool restaurant. In her 1966 Swinging London article for *Time* magazine, Piri Halasz describes five 'scenes' in the groovy capital. 'SCENE THREE' takes place at Le Reve, where actors Terence Stamp and Michael Caine, hairdresser Vidal Sassoon, photographer David Bailey and tailor Doug Hayward are discussing the evils of apartheid and the fortunes of Chelsea FC. It is Saturday and they are having a quick lunch before going to a match at Stamford Bridge. One of them tells the young American journalist that this 'joke team' has started playing well and they are thinking of switching their allegiances to Fulham. Apparently, they did so, because in Halasz's 1967 follow-up book, *A Swinger's Guide to London*, 'Mike Caine,' Vidal Sasson and Terence Stamp have another quick Saturday lunch there before going to see Fulham play at Craven Cottage.

Of the characters present at Halasz's first lunch, perhaps only Doug Hayward (1934–2008) needs an introduction. He is alleged to have provided the inspiration for Michael Caine's *Alfie* (in the famous 1966 movie of the same name) and for Geoffrey Rush's Harry Pendel in *The Tailor of Panama* (the 2001 film adaptation of a John Le Carré story). Hayward is listed in *The New London Spy* (1966) as a tailor whose clients are 'well-groomed actors and socialites'. His phone number is given as 'FUL 6179' and we learn that his hand-tailored suits could cost anything from 60 guineas.

Halasz (1967) describes Le Reve as 'a cheapish jolly Frenchy little place, with surrealistic canvasses on the wall'.

Le Reve.

## The Casserole and the Gigolo Club
## No. 338 King's Road
## London, SW3 5UR

Duggie Fields said that 'the Casserole was a lunchtime restaurant. Paloma Picasso used to go there, as did Loulou de la Falaise. So it attracted a lot of Europeans to it, too. And below the Casserole there was a gay night club called The Gigolo'.

Paloma Picasso, who was born in 1949, is the youngest daughter of Pablo Picasso and is a fashion designer, as was Loulou de la Falaise (1948–2011).

According to *Len Deighton's London Dossier* (1967) the ballet dancer Rudolf Nureyev was also a client of the Casserole. The book called it a 'superior bistro,' although it warned readers that the waiters were likely to lean their 'dainty hips' against the table 'while taking your order'. It also informed potential visitors that membership of the Gigolo Club was exclusively male, and that it was better not to go 'down there if you like women'. According to Halasz (1967), the Casserole was 'chic and pleasant, though situated in the midst of fairyland'. Before judging these comments by today's standards, perhaps we should remember that homophobia was pretty much the norm at that time: 1967 saw the passage of the Sexual Offences Act, which finally legalised homosexual acts in private between consenting males over the age of twenty-one.

The Casserole and the Gigolo Club.

# SW5

## The Troubadour
## No. 265 Old Brompton Road
## London, SW5 9JA

The Troubadour first opened for business in 1954 and was associated with the beatnik generation. For Piri Halasz (1967) it was a survivor of the time 'five or six years ago' when London was 'sprouting coffee bars the way it's bursting out in discotheques now'. Yet James Clough, who was an art student in the 1960s, has fond memories: 'You could play chess there, there were poetry readings and jazz evenings as well. It was very nice.'

The Troubadour was set up by 'Mike Blumen, a voluble, shaggy-haired Montrealer of Dutch-Irish ancestry' (Halasz) and his wife Sheila, and they were to run the show until 1972. Dallas and Fantoni (1967), who list it in both their restaurants and folk section, call the couple 'Van Bloemen'. They also tell us that it is 'the country's oldest folk club' and that 'most of the big folk who hit London sing at the the Troub'. Bob Dylan played here during his first visit to the UK in late 1962/early 1963, as did Paul Simon a couple of years later. The not very folky Jimi Hendrix was also a regular during his time in London.

Concerts took place in the basement on Tuesday and Saturday nights (when copies of *The Observer* were on sale there ahead of its Sunday publication). The ground floor was a coffee bar that opened every day at 11 a.m.

The Troubadour.

# SW7

## No. 31 Montpelier Square
## London, SW7 1JY

'SCENE FIVE' in Piri Halasz's Swinging London article (*Time*, 1966) describes a Saturday night party at 'a brightly lit Georgian house in Kensington,' with a guest list that includes Marlon Brando, Prince Stanislas Radziwill and Lee (Bouvier Canfield), Roddy McDowall, Terry Southern, Francoise Sagan, Barbra Streisand and Warren Beatty. It is the home of thirty-four-year-old Leslie Caron who, we learn, is 'unquestionably this season's most with-it hostess'. Halasz discreetly avoids giving an address, although it was in fact No. 31 Montpelier Square, a very 'des res' a few hundred yards to the north of Harrods.

Leslie Caron was a French actress who had recently divorced her second husband – theatre director Peter Hall. They had two small children and she kept the house. Beatty was in fact cited as a co-respondent in their divorce case.

Montpelier Square.

Cranley Mansion.

## Cranley Mansion
## No. 160 Gloucester Road
## London, SW7 4QF

According to Jenny Fabian, Cranley Mansion, on the corner of Gloucester Road and the Old Brompton Road, was the site of an entertaining literary salon. It was in this late Victorian building (1885) that a young writer with a drug serious habit, Thom Keyes, occupied a large flat. Keyes, a public schoolboy and Oxford graduate, had become a minor celebrity with his novel *All Night Stand* (1966), about the sexual antics of a Liverpool rock group. He later became a screenplay writer and this could explain his friendship with *Performance* co-director Donald Cammell.

Fabian recalls:

> Thommy Keyes's flat in South Kensington, which was a great hub of all the hip intelligentsia of that era, meeting, like Donald Cammell, Roman Polanski, all those sort of people. You'd go round and there'd always be somebody interesting from the underground: Steve Abrams, Yul Brynner even appeared one day! Because Thommy had great associations with Hollywood and also was friends with this amazing guy called Melvin Abner Fishman, who produced the *Steppenwolf* film (1974).

Abrams, an American who ran a parapsychology laboratory at Oxford, was the founder of SOMA (Society of Mental Awareness) and the author of the full-page ad calling for cannabis law reform that appeared in *The Times* on Monday 24 July 1967. Abrams died in 2012. Brynner (1985), Keyes (1995) and Cammell (1996) predeceased him.

## The Royal Albert Hall
## Kensington Gore
## London, SW7 2AP

If the Roundhouse played a role in the birth of London's underground scene, then so did another Victorian edifice, the Royal Albert Hall. Almost a century after its inauguration (in 1871) it hosted the International Poetry Incarnation, which took place on Friday 11 June 1965.

The Royal Albert Hall.

The catalyst had been the arrival in London the previous month of the Beat poet Allen Ginsberg. Ginsberg had turned up at Better Books and had offered to read for free 'anywhere'. This noble gesture prompted (Barry) Miles to make the even nobler gesture of organising the event. Miles did so rapidly and managed to assemble an impressive collection of performers from both sides of the Atlantic. They included Ginsberg's fellow Beats Lawrence Ferlinghetti, Gregory Corso and William Burroughs, while the British contingent included Adrian Mitchell, George Macbeth, Alexander Trocchi, Michael Horovitz and Christopher Logue. Estimates of the audience size vary from 5,000 to 7,000.

And yet the event had its drawbacks. Miles recalls:

Although it was a fantastic coming together of the tribes, as it were, as a reading it wasn't very good: Ginsberg got drunk, Corso for some reason chose to read sitting down, even though he was in the centre of a circular building, and read a long, difficult poem about LSD; rather than one of his rabble-rousing, you know, Hair, or Marriage, or one of those. As a poetry reading, it wasn't great.

Nevertheless, it is generally considered to have been a key moment in the story of Swinging London. The event was recorded for posterity in Peter Whitehead's 33-minute documentary, *Wholly Communion.*

The International Poetry Incarnation also helped pave the way for the Royal Albert Hall to become a significant rock concert venue. Acts who played there in the 1960s included Pink Floyd, who were still largely unknown when they joined Peter Cook and Dudley Moore and others in 'You're Joking', an Oxfam charity concert, on Monday 12 December 1966, and who were less obscure when featured in the line-up for a Jimi Hendrix concert on Tuesday 14 November 1967. The following year the Hall had the rare distinction of hosting Cream's two farewell concerts and the Eurovision Song Contest. And, last but not least, the Who and Chuck Berry performed there on Saturday 5 July 1969, a few hours after the 'Stones in the Park' concert in nearby Hyde Park.

# Flat 1
# Egerton Court
# Nos 6–8 Old Brompton Road
# London, SW7 3HT

Egerton Court is a large, white, semicircular building across the road from South Kensington Underground station. In the 1960s at least one of its flats functioned as the digs for some film

Egerton Court.

students at the Royal College of Art. They included Storm Thorgerson, Aubrey 'Po' Powell, David Gale and David Henderson. Thorgerson and Powell would go on to form the Hipgnosis design company, which was responsible for a number of iconic rock album covers. Their starting point was Pink Floyd, some of whose members Storm Thorgerson had known from his youth in Cambridge. And it was at Egerton Court that Storm was invited to design the cover for the band's second album, 1968's *A Saucerful of Secrets*. He recalled:

> Somebody in the next room in the apartment I lived in, when I was a student, was asked by the Pink Floyd to do a cover and refused. And I was listening at the door, right? And I heard him refuse, so I said, 'I'll do that!' and the band said, 'Oh, OK.' I mean, we knew each other, so they just thought I was being nosey, but they didn't want the record company to do it, so they wanted one of their own people to do it, and that happened to be me, so that's by luck, I didn't know I was going to do this.

In 1968 the merry band at Egerton Court was joined by two more young people from Cambridge: London School of Film Technique student Nigel Lesmoir-Gordon and his girlfriend, Jenny, who had previously lived at No. 101 Cromwell Road. They were friends with Mick Jagger and Marianne Faithfull, who used to visit. Nigel recalled:

> I remember one night Marianne was there and Jenny and me and a couple of other people, and we were tripping in our beautiful oval-shaped room and it had these enormous windows that look right out onto the South Ken complex, so you would stand at these windows like some aristocrat and survey the world beneath you!

> Mick came round to get Marianne and we let him in and he came into the room and he looked rather put out and shy and awkward, so he went and stood downstairs – well, I found him downstairs on the staircase sort of with his head in his hands, and I said, 'What's the matter? What's the matter?' And he said, 'Well, I don't know, you're all doing something and I don't know half the people and I feel awkward, so...' I said, 'Oh, you don't have to be awkward, just come in, you know just pop in for a minute, and if you want, we'll go out.'

And another Cambridge character, Ian Moore, or 'Imo', was also present. As for Mick Jagger, Nigel said:

He came in and sat for a while, and he said, 'Look, my car's outside, why don't we go up to Primrose Hill? You know, you, Jenny, Marianne, me and we'll squeeze Imo in as well.' So we all went down and outside Egerton Court was this most beautiful Aston Martin. And Jenny and I hadn't even got a car, let alone an Aston Martin, so that was quite nice. But then we all piled in and then, what really blew my mind was Mick picked up a 45 RPM, a little, you know 7-inch disc, and under the dashboard was a 45 RPM player, the height of luxury! I didn't know a 45 RPM car device even existed, but he had one and he actually played some Rolling Stones going up there. It might even have been Ruby Tuesday.

'Ruby Tuesday' was released as a single in 1967. Nigel and Jenny left Egerton Court at some stage in 1968 in order to go on the hippy trail to India. Their room was taken by another friend from Cambridge: Syd Barrett, who had begun to outstay his welcome both at No. 101 Cromwell Road and in Pink Floyd. Stories abound of his increasingly strange behaviour at Egerton Court. In late 1969 he moved to Wetherby Mansions in Earls Court, where he shared a flat with Duggie Fields.

It's said that other people who lived in flats at Egerton Court at the time included Roger Dean, the man who did for Yes what Storm Thorgerson did for Pink Floyd, and the photographer Mick Rock (who took the cover photo for Barrett's 1970 album *The Madcap Laughs* at the aforementioned flat in Earls Court).

## The Cromwellian

## No. 3 Cromwell Road

## London, SW7 2HR

George Melly visited the Cromwellian (cocktail bar and discotheque) at No. 103 Cromwell Road in the autumn of 1965 (as part of his research for an article that was later reproduced in his 1970 book *Revolt into Style*) and interviewed the general manager, Bart Kimber. Melly claimed that the club was not as 'in' as it had been six months previously, and Kimber seemed quite happy with this state of affairs. He told Melly: 'Look, of course we're successful. Parking's easy out here and you can get stoned out of your eyeballs for £2. We don't want to be in.' (Presumably in 1965 'stoned' still referred to inebriation and not the effects of marijuana.)

The Cromwellian.

And yet the Cromwellian continued to be fairly in. According to Halasz (1967) it was popular with 'younger pop stars who are only just beginning to make it'. When reminiscing many years later about London in the 1960s, Brian Auger recalled:

> It was like a big family of musicians. Everybody knew everyone anyway, and so people would just turn up and in some of the clubs like the Cromwellian, everybody made for that club after they'd finished their gigs at the Ricky-Tick [in Windsor], or whatever it was. And so there'd be like basically the Who's Who in London at that place, and also at Blaises, just around the corner in Queen's Gate, and the Bags of Nails, of course.

The Cromwellian had great showcase potential, which, says Brian Auger, is why Jimi Hendrix played there in 1966. Auger was approached by Chas Chandler and asked to let this unknown guitarist front his new band – Trinity. He was naturally reluctant but suggested that Hendrix might like to jam with them the following Friday.

> At the Cromwellian we play our set and we get to the break and Chas brings Jimi over, and Jimi's a really nice guy. He said: 'Yeah, I'd love to sit in with you' and I said, 'Fine, man. What do you want to play?' And he said: 'Well, can you play this chord sequence?' And he shows me this sequence of chords, which were for Hey Joe. Actually, I found out afterwards because I didn't know Hey Joe anyway, but the sequence was pretty straightforward. So I said: 'Yeah, we could do that. Just count the tempo in and we'll let fly.' And so he counted the tempo in and when he started to play we were just floored because none of us had heard anything like that!

Other musicians who are believed to have played at the Cromwellian include Reg Dwight (aka Elton John), Georgie Fame, Eric Burdon (Chandler's former band mate in the Animals), Eric Clapton and – once – blues legend Sonny Boy Williamson. Yet music was only part of the entertainment in this three-storey terraced house. The musical club/bar/disco was in the cellar, while the Armoury Bar (or 'Harry's Bar', run by Harry Heart) was on the ground floor, and there was a small gambling casino (and another bar) on the first floor. Brian Epstein was known to frequent the casino, while the Beatles occasionally hung out in the cellar. Their presence is confirmed in *The New London Spy* (1966), which reminds visitors of the 'rule of the house: no autographs'. It also advises them not to go 'looking for punch-ups' as five of the six directors are professional wrestlers. One of these, Bob Anthony (real name Bob Archer), was in charge of running the disco and booking the bands.

According to *Len Deighton's London Dossier*, the Cromwellian had begun to lose its shine by 1967. In the chapter on 'Teenagers' Jane Wilson claimed that the Ad Lib had originally been the 'in' place, followed by the Scotch of St James and, 'very briefly,' the Cromwellian, having been replaced by Dolly's 'at the time of writing'.

# Blaises

# No. 121 Queen's Gate

# London, SW7

Speaking in 2006, Anita Pallenberg said, 'I can vaguely remember Blaises, which I think was on Exhibition Road. And I remember seeing the Pink Floyd there a lot and they would do their light shows there and I was kind of fascinated by that. I liked to go there. It was kind of like my favourite club.'

The club wasn't far from the flat that she shared with Brian Jones at No. 1 Courtfield Road. Indeed, Blaises, like Anita Pallenberg, looms large in the story of the Rolling Stones. It is believed that the Redlands bust at Keith Richard's Sussex home in February 1967 was retaliation (by the

Blaises.

*News of the World*, in collaboration with the police) for Mick Jagger's announcement (made on the Eamonn Andrews Show one week earlier) that he intended to sue the paper for libel. This was after it had accused him of taking LSD (in the company of the Moody Blues). It had also alleged that Jagger had been overheard discussing his drug habit one evening at Blaises, but, as Mick Farren explained, it was a case of mistaken identity:

'Brian Jones was down there and he was kind of drunk and mouthing off and typical... well, it wasn't Murdoch then, but the same sort of tabloid stupidity, the guy thought he was talking to Mick Jagger. So he credited all this nonsense that Brian was coming out with about drugs and girls and sex and whatever, it was Jagger saying it, and basically they had them dead to rights.' But the Redlands bust and the subsequent trial changed all that: 'After the Redlands bust, the case against the *News of the World* became kind of academic. I mean, it still could have proceeded ahead, it was all a bit sort of Oscar Wilde-like.'

Apart from its Pink Floyd and Rolling Stones associations, Blaises was a cool hangout in its own right. It is one of the fifteen 'discotheques' listed by Dallas and Fantoni (1967). They tell us that membership cost 2 guineas, while food was 'about £1' and that there were 'live groups, gambling'. Halasz (1967) described it as 'near the Cromwellian and somewhat tidier, but also cheapish and jolly and informal'.

## No. 1 Courtfield Road
## London, SW7 4DD

Brian Jones and Anita Pallenberg lived in a flat here from 1966 to 1967. And, as Keith Richards explains in his autobiography, *Life*, he was a regular guest, often staying the night. He confesses that this marked the start of his own relationship with Pallenberg, even though this didn't become a fully fledged affair until later, when they were being chauffeur-driven to Morocco.

Keith and Anita subsequently became a famous rock couple. Pallenberg had a fling with Mick Jagger when they were working on the cult '60s movie *Performance*, while Richards, who seems to enjoy telling the story in *Life*, returned the favour by seducing (or being seduced by) Jagger's then girlfriend, Marianne Faithfull.

Anita Pallenberg, who acted in another famous '60s movie, *Barbarella*, with Jane Fonda, didn't have particularly fond memories of life in Courtfield Road. After all, this was the age of Beatlemania, and the Stones had their fair share of unduly enthusiastic female fans. She recalled:

There were the girls who would sit outside the house and wait. If I would come out, or if Brian would go out, they'd say, 'Can we make his bed, can we make you a cup of tea? Can we do

No. 1 Courtfield Road.

anything, just to get in the house?' And then I said, 'OK, make a cup of tea' and they made us a cup of tea, and then they asked me if they could do the bed. And I said, 'OK,' but I mean, shouldn't have really, I should have kept them away more.

On at least one occasion things got quite nasty:

The only time I called the police in England was because I had these girls who were kind of abusing me. It must have been like 2 o'clock in the morning, and they were shouting abuse at me and I just couldn't take it any longer. I threw water over them and they still carried on, and eventually I just had them removed by the cops, but it was a pretty aggressive type of woman. Nowadays I see all these young girls kind of going to pubs, and the yob culture, and it's a bit similar, it's only that they seem to have put their interests into other things – thank God! – but we were pretty much the target of all those kind of girls.

Anita Pallenberg left Brian Jones for Keith Richards in 1967. The following year she moved in with him when he bought a home in Cheyne Walk, while Brian Jones acquired Cotchford Farm in Sussex. This was better known as 'The House at Pooh Corner', having been the home of the writer A. A. Milne and his son Christopher Robin. Jones drowned in the house's swimming pool, in mysterious circumstances, on Thursday 3 July 1969. He was twenty-seven.

No. 1 Courtfield Road was an impressive building and it is now part of the Millennium Bailey's Hotel, even though the hotel's official address is No. 140 Gloucester Road.

# No. 101 Cromwell Road
# London, SW7 4DN

'Most of the LSD in London made its way out into the world through Cromwell Road, through 101, so a lot of people were coming to 101 to get their LSD and it kind of, in a way, spread out and it attracted people who were on the quest for knowledge and understanding. It attracted poets, musicians, writers.'

As former No. 101 Cromwell Road resident Nigel Lesmoir-Gordon observed, the house had a certain standing in the counter-culture world. Donovan even described its activities in his song 'Sunny South Kensington', which appeared on his 1967 album *Yellow Mellow* (which was released in the USA, but not in the UK, for contractual reasons). Donovan was a regular visitor to No. 101 and, as Nigel Lesmoir-Gordon (who had moved to London from Cambridge in 1965 in order to study film, having previously attended Oundle, a famous boarding school in Northamptonshire) says, there were plenty of others: 'Allen Ginsberg was a visitor, Mick Jagger was a visitor, P.B. Proby, even the amazing Vince Taylor came there. Vince Taylor and the Playboys were an English leather rock band that we listened to at Oundle, and he was tripping. Actually, he tripped out too much, I think, because he went to France as Vince Taylor and came back as Matheus the son of God!'

The artist Duggie Fields, who abandoned architecture school in order to go to art college, also lived at No. 101, which was a large four-storey house with numerous residents. He said that the address had a certain name recognition:

> There was a period where one could sort of a flag a taxi down in the street. Now, we had no money, but we did travel by taxi quite a lot. And we'd flag a taxi down and say, '101…' and they'd look at us and go 'Cromwell Road,' and that happened on quite a few occasions. Other times American sort of hippie tourists would sort of follow people into the building: 'Gee, you guys look so cute, can we do anything for you? You know, can we we buy you any food? Can we clean up for you?' sort of thing.

Nigel Lesmoir-Gordon had more to say about the American guests:

> Burroughs came to 101 and in fact he said to me, 'Nigel, you've got to stop taking this LSD!' I said, 'That's a bit rich coming from you, William!' But still, I ignored him. There were a lot of American poets, artists, musicians who came. Kenneth Anger came there, showed his films. A lot of people came there who were actually on the run from the Vietnam War, from conscription, who connected, through 101, to the sub-culture.

England's own Pink Floyd also had a No. 101 connection. Roger Waters briefly lived there, as did Syd Barrett, who started to behave erratically at about this time, probably on account of his acid consumption. New Zealander John Esam, a self-styled 'LSD evangelist,' was also a No. 101 resident. Barrett fled to Egerton Court in 1968.

No. 101 Cromwell Road's interesting residents and guests even led Yoko Ono to pay a visit in 1967, as Duggie Fields recalled: 'I remember once someone said, "Yoko Ono's downstairs, she's looking for people to be in her *Bottoms* film. Will you do it?" And I said, "No." And I was painting upstairs and I didn't go down. I never met her. I saw the *Bottoms* film at the Serpentine summer show, and I thought, "I could have been one of them!"'

The No. 101 building is no more: it was demolished in order to make way for the Kensington Holiday Inn, which is listed at No. 97 Cromwell Road.

No. 101 Cromwell Road.

# SW10

## The Baghdad House
## No. 140 Fulham Road
## London, SW10 9PY

Paul McCartney once dined at the Baghdad House with Andy Warhol (whom he described as 'lovely'), while Mick Jagger often went there with Marianne Faithfull, James Fox (with whom Jagger starred in *Performance*) and his girlfriend, Andee Cohen. In September 1967 Mick and Marianne ate at the Baghdad House with the famous fashion photographer Cecil Beaton (Beaton was now in his sixties and his friendship with Jagger and Richards, who were still in their twenties, prompted the critic Cyril Connolly to nickname him 'Rip-Van-With-It'). Other Baghdad House regulars included Donovan and Georgie Fame.

The distinguished clientele also attracted Jenny Fabian, who recalls:

You just went downstairs and – was he called Ahmed? He could have been called anything! – but anyway he used to bring you these delicious… of course, don't forget hummus would have been a novelty in those days! So that was the first taste of hummus and pittas. And you just sat on these cushions at these wonderful tables and ate this exotic food and interesting people would float in and out of it. Not necessarily… I can't name who these interesting people are, but anybody who came there was obviously interesting and to be ogled at, and, hopefully, you were as interesting as they were, too. So it was that: if you knew where to go, the people there would probably be interesting.

Artist Duggie Fields was also a fan. He said:

There was a downstairs with cushions on the floor. It was the first place that I ever saw that was ethnically themed, shall we say? I'd never been anywhere like that, and I think most people hadn't. There were people going to Marrakesh for the first time: and I never went. So the Baghdad House was a hang-out and you could go and there would be people there, other people one would know, people on the scene, there would be people making music.

Fields added:

A lot of smoking joints there too. If they knew you, they would sort of lock the door once you were in. You know, this was in the period when a small possession of hash could have you in jail, but the

The Baghdad House.

> Baghdad House was quite relaxed on that level and quite friendly and we would frequently go with no money, and expect someone to pick up the bill, or I do remember them saying, 'Well, just pay us when you can.'

In his memoir *White Bicycles: Making Music in the 1960s* Joe Boyd recalls that the Baghdad House was 'adored' by both the music business and the criminal fraternity, specifying that they were 'often quite different people'.

Boyd says that the Baghdad House was run by 'an enigmatic Iraqi and his red-haired Scottish girlfriend,' while another account has it the managers were two Moroccan brothers. Given the name, the enigmatic Iraqi theory is more plausible.

# Hung on You (2)
# No. 430 King's Road
# London, SW10 0LJ

According to the *Gear Guide 1967*, this was the location of 4.30, a 'Mostly Girls' shop run by Carol Derry, 'a very charming young woman' but towards the end of the year it was replaced by Michael Rainey's Hung on You, which moved there from No. 22 Cale Street. And yet, as Rainey's wife, Jane Ormsby-Gore, said in an interview at the Victoria & Albert Museum in 2006, 'Michael made the most gigantic mistake of leaving Cale Street and going onto the King's Road. He felt that it was happening on the King's Road, but it cost a lot of money to move, and people didn't know where we were. It became less successful then.'

Rainey and Gore sold the lease to Trevor Roberts in 1969. He changed the name to Mr Freedom. In 1971 it became Paradise Garage, and it was here that Malcolm McLaren and Vivienne Westwood sold 1950s rock 'n' roll clothing. McLaren himself took over the premises in late '71 and changed the name – first to Let it Rock and later Sex – and it became a popular hangout for the future members of the Sex Pistols and other young punks. Today No. 430 King's Road goes by the name of World's End and is still owned by Vivienne Westwood.

Hung on You, No. 430 King's Road.

## The Flying Dragon
## No. 434 King's Road
## London, SW10 0LJ

In the words of Duggie Fields: 'Then there was Hung on You, also on the corner, just where the Vivienne Westwood shop is. And for a while there was the Dragon café next door, which had a big dragon painted on the window and clouds on the ceiling, moving clouds painted on the ceiling with a projector, and that was a sort of cushion on the floor sort of hang-out.'

Jenny Fabian agrees that it was 'down towards the bottom of the Kings Road, on the bend'. She adds: 'But the Flying Dragon was just this room full of cushions and everybody sitting round, as Jonathan Meades described it, "like aspirant vegetables".'

The Flying Dragon's artwork was by an organisation called Om Tentacle, which was a partnership between Mike McInnerney, the art editor at *The International Times*, and Dudley Edwards. As Edwards explains in an interview in Norman Hathaway and Dan Nadel's book, *Electrical Banana: Masters of Psychedelic Art*, he had previously been part of the Binder, Edwards & Vaughan design group. The three partners had met at Bradford Art College in the early 1960s and moved to London. Here, from 1965 onwards, their psychedelic paintwork (which included a car that appeared on the cover of the Kinks's 1966 album *Sunny Afternoon*, Tara Browne's AC 'Shelby' Cobra, the shopfront of

The Flying Dragon.

Dandie Fashions on the King's Road, a similar commission at Lord John in Carnaby Street, and Paul McCartney's piano) led to them being considered 'the Beatles of the art world,' but they went their separate ways in 1967. The Flying Dragon mural was created in 1968. In his interview in the book Edwards admits that Om Tentacle didn't have a car at first, but that Jane Asher kindly gave them her old Ford. He adds: 'She wouldn't take any money for it, so we gave her a wooden statue of Shiva.'

In actual fact the Flying Dragon wasn't next door to Hung on You, but was two doors down at No. 434 King's Road.

## Granny Takes a Trip
## No. 488 King's Road
## London, SW10 0LF

This psychedelic unisex shop in World's End was one of three establishments to be included under the heading 'Way Out' in the otherwise conservative chapter on men's clothes in *The New London Spy* (1966) – the other two were Hung on You and Just Men (in Tryon Street). And that is a fair reflection on its importance as 'the place' – at least in sartorial terms. Its coolness was such that it even became the title of a song, which was released by the Purple Gang in 1967.

Accounts vary regarding the shop's opening date, from December 1965 to February 1966, and it was sufficiently well established to appear in 'SCENE TWO: Saturday Afternoon in Chelsea' in Piri Halasz's Swinging London article for *Time* magazine (April 1966). Its three founders were Nigel Waymouth; his girlfriend Sheila Cohen, who had a vast collection of Victorian clothes; and John Pearse, a tailor who had 'dropped out' of Savile Row. Pearse was also a lover of all things Victorian and found inspiration at an Aubrey Beardsley exhibition at the V&A in 1966. He also liked the fabric designs of William Morris and used them to create jackets. The fact that he used materials like velvet and satin, which were normally intended for curtains and which he bought at Liberty's, was one of the reasons why Granny Takes a Trip was an expensive place.

All of the Beatles shopped there, as did Jimi Hendrix and various members of the Rolling Stones, as well as Anita Pallenberg, the Who, Pink Floyd and the Small Faces. Future celebrities associated with it included Salman Rushdie, who lived in a flat above the shop, and a young designer called Paul Smith who occasionally bought clothes there when he 'had the money.'

Granny Takes a Trip was also famous for its exterior, which constantly changed, featuring, at various stages, Native American chief Kicking Bear, Jean Harlow and a (real) 1968 Dodge. According to the shop's advertising, it sold 'clothes to wear before you make love' and there was a rumour that if you licked the label on them, you could begin your own acid trip.

Granny Takes a Trip.

In 1969 Waymouth, Cohen and Pearse sold the business to its manager, Freddie Hornik, who carried on serving the rich and famous until closing the shop in the 1970s.

## No. 100 Cheyne Walk
## London, SW10 0DQ

'On Cheyne Walk Christopher Gibbs had a wonderful apartment where a scene in *Blow-Up* was filmed. It took them three days to film those few seconds in the film.'

So says Prince Stanislas Klossowski de Rola, better known as 'Stash de Rola'. De Rola, the son of the painter Balthus, and Christopher Gibbs (1938–2018), an Old Etonian antiques dealer, had a lot in common: they were both aristocratic aesthetes and friends of rock stars, whom they often advised on sartorial matters. Therefore it wasn't surprising that 'Stash' was at the party that would be used in Michelangelo Antonioni's cult 1966 movie. He recalls:

> And the production bought an awful amount of drugs and tons of booze, they didn't want any extras, they wanted real people, so they paid everybody incredible sums. I think it was 100 quid per night, which was a huge amount of money in those days, when people made £15 a week and so on. And basically one made £300 in three nights just to hang around and smoke dope and drink and be present, you know, for a split second of being on the screen, in my case.

Which was? 'If you freeze-frame you can see me with Michael Rainey, as David Hemmings comes in. I was near the entrance, so the camera sort of pans past me. There's a couple of shots. You kind of get glimpses, but you'd have to freeze-frame to see me in it.'

Nor was the party scene in *Blow-Up* No. 100 Cheyne Walk's only claim to fame. Mick Jagger became a neighbour when he and his girlfriend Marianne Faithfull into a house at No. 48. Gibbs helped them decorate. According to Christopher Andersen's 2012 biography, *Mick: The Wild Life and Mad Genius of Jagger*, Mick and Marianne attended a party chez Gibbs in 1967. The guest list included Princess Margaret, Allen Ginsberg, John Paul Getty II (another neighbour), as well as assorted lords and ladies. According to Anderson, a butler served hash on a silver tray. Unfortunately, cook had accidentally doubled the amount of hashish and many guests, including Princess Margaret, were rushed to hospital with 'food poisoning'.

No. 100 Cheyne Walk was also used as a location in Kenneth Anger's satanic short *Lucifer Rising*, which was shot between 1966 and 1972. The cast included Marianne Faithfull, Jimmy Page, Chris Jagger, Donald Cammell and Manson murderer Bobby Beausoleil.

No. 100 Cheyne Walk.

# SE7

## Maryon Park
## London, SE7

Maryon Park in Charlton in southeast London appears in some key scenes in Antonioni's 1966 film *Blow-Up*. It is here that Thomas (David Hemmings) furtively snaps Jane (Vanessa Redgrave) without her permission. Later, when he 'blows up' the photo back at his studio, he realises that part of a body is hidden in the park's undergrowth. And when Thomas returns to the 'scene of the crime' he witnesses a mimed game of tennis.

Maryon Park is named after Sir Spencer Maryon Wilson, the man who donated the land to London County Council for the park, which opened in 1890. The area had once been known as the Hanging Wood, as highwaymen operated there and whenever they were caught it was also where they were hanged. The land was later occupied by the Charlton sandpits, and one of these was covered to create the park. Another pit in the neighbourhood was filled in by a volunteer army of Charlton Athletic fans to create the club's ground, The Valley, in 1919.

According to an article in *The Independent* in 2006, published on the 40th anniversary of *Blow-Up,* there were two possible explanations as to why Antonioni had chosen this park in a rather out of the way part of town. One was that it was at a unique confluence of ley lines; the other was that it was quiet.

The park hasn't changed much since Antonioni's day. The tennis court is easy to find, and the other locations are recognisable.

Maryon Park.

# EC2

## The Antiuniversity of London
## No. 49 Rivington Street
## London, EC2A 3QB

The Antiuniversity of London opened on Monday 12 February 1968 in premises at No. 49 Rivington Street in Shoreditch. Yet this was not the building's first association with alternative culture. According to James Clough, who was then an art student, 'The Bertrand Russell Peace Foundation was there and the Vietnam Solidarity Committee was there. They had the whole building, it was about two or three floors. It was a quiet part of London.' He started working there and designed for the anti-Vietnam War protest march on Sunday 22 October 1967. The poster gives No. 49 Rivington Street as the address of the organisers, 'the October 22nd Vietnam ad hoc Cttee.'

Clough adds: 'And I can remember somebody invited me for a drink in the pub below [the Bricklayers Arms] and it became very clear that he was a cop looking for information, and trying to see how much he could get from me. And I was young and perhaps ingenuous and maybe they thought they could worm out some information from me!'

The Antiuniversity opened four months later. There were 'no formal requirements' for attendance and, according to Richard Whitmore's report for BBC News, 'Getting into the Antiuniversity is mainly a question of finding out where it is.' The general idea was to 'offer new-style courses in contemporary arts, politics and psychology,' although specific areas of study included 'black power, counter-culture and revolution. Signing on costs £8, plus 10 shillings for each course you attend.' Its founders included Marxist economist Allen Krebs, who had previously been involved in FUNY (the Free University of New York); John Latham, 'who left a London art school after returning a library book in a test tube of acid'; and David Cooper, a South African psychiatrist who invented the term 'anti-psychiatry'. The university faculty included *Naked Lunch* author William Burroughs, Black Panther Stokely Carmichael, artists Jim Dine and Richard Hamilton, *International Times* founders Jim Haynes and (Barry) Miles, Cooper's fellow anti-psychiatrist and Philadelphia Association member R. D. Laing, poets Allen Ginsberg and Adrian Henri (spelt 'Henry' on the poster) and authors C. L. R. James, Jeff Nuttall and Alexander Trocchi. The few female faculty members listed included musician Annea Lockwood, psychoanalyst Juliet Mitchell, artist Carolee Schneemann and author Susan Sherman.

The Antiuniversity of London.

# EC4

## *News of the World*
## No. 65 Fleet Street
## London, EC4Y 1HS

'We basically picketed the *News of the World* building after they'd stitched up Mick Jagger and Keith Richards.'

This is how Mick Farren introduced the events that took place in Fleet Street during the last week of June 1967. The protest followed the conviction of Jagger and Richards on Thursday 29 June. This was at the end of the trial for the Redlands bust in February, in which the police, in collusion with the *News of the World*, had raided Keith Richards's Sussex home.

After the verdict was announced the hippy community mobilised and some 1,500 'freaks' gathered outside the *News of the World* building, something for which the police were not prepared. The protesters enlisted the services of Karl Dallas, a Marxist who worked as a journalist in both the music and fashion world. He recalled:

> When the *News of the World* persecuted Mick Jagger, the hippy underground decided to organise a blockade, to stop them getting the newsprint in, so they rang me up because they knew of my political background. They said: 'How do we organise a demonstration, Karl?' So I gave them a few tips, but when the demonstration took place, I'd been working in some fashion industry exercise, so I was wearing my Savile Row suit etc. and I went along to the demo, which totally confused the policeman because he said, 'Are you part of this demonstration, or just a bystander, sir?' I said, 'I'm part of the demonstration.' 'So get on the fucking pavement!' he said.

Mick Farren said that the demonstrators soon found a way to thwart the police:

> No sooner had the cops cleared off the street one time, everybody came back because we realised they were letting the buses go on through, because I mean there's a lot of buses go down Fleet Street. So all you had to do was jump on a bus, but as soon as the police lined up, and you were back where you started from. I mean it was really the only riot I've ever been to that was conducted by London Transport, literally!

But the police became more savvy over the next few days. The following evening (Friday 30 June) revellers left the UFO and marched to Piccadilly Circus, where the police and their dogs were waiting for them. On Saturday (1 July) between 2,000 and 3,000 people gathered at No. 65 Fleet

*News of the World.*

Street, with the aim of blocking the *News of the World* (a Sunday paper). Again, they received a hostile reception.

Mick Farren was considered a ringleader and therefore got dragged into an alley and 'worked over' by the police. He saw the demonstration and the Redlands bust as part of a larger battle:

> And supposedly, you know, the rumour at the time was that it was a rehearsal for getting the Beatles. I mean, people don't sort of think about this anymore, but they wanted to stamp us out. I mean, they wanted this stuff to stop, they wanted it to go away, they wanted everything to go back to, you know, that we should all be schoolboys like Jennings and Darbishire and then go in the RAF and be Biggles or something. It was really like turning back time, but they didn't see it that way.

The *News of the World*, which was founded in 1843, left Fleet Street for Wapping in 1986. Its owner, Rupert Murdoch, decided to suspend publication in 2011 in the wake of the phone-hacking scandal.

# E3

**Kingsley Hall**

**Powis Road**

**London, E3 3HJ**

From 1965 to 1970 Kingsley Hall was used by the Glaswegian psychiatrist R. D. Laing (1927–89) and the Philadelphia Association for an unusual experiment. A community was set up in which schizophrenic patients lived alongside therapists, the idea being that it would be hard to tell them apart. In his 1968 book *Bomb Culture*, Jeff Nuttall (1933–2004) made numerous references to this 'community for regenerative madness'. If *Bomb Culture* is considered a major 1960s text, then so is Laing's own book, *The Divided Self*, which was published in 1960.

Kingsley Hall had an interesting history prior to Laing. It had been set up as a community centre in honour of Kingsley Lester, a young man who had died in1914 and whose sisters ran a local primary school. He left money for a centre, which became known as 'Kingsley Hall' and moved to its current premises in 1928. In 1931 Mahatma Gandhi stayed there for several months and even received a visit from Charlie Chaplin. Some of the Jarrow Crusade marchers were offered hospitality there when they reached London in 1936.

The hall fell into disuse when the Philadelphia Association left in 1970, but it was revived in 1982 when Richard Attenborough used it to film some scenes for Gandhi. The centre reopened in 1985.

Kingsley Hall.

# NW1

## St Pancras Station
## Pancras Road
## London, NW1 2QP

St Pancras station was the setting for an interesting '60s moment. In 1968, 100 years after it opened, a high priest and 150 young people in flowing robes gathered here under the moonlight. They wanted to levitate the station and move it to Bermondsey. According to an account published in *The Evening Standard* on Tuesday 8 October that year, the assembled 'hippies' chanted to the accompaniment of violins, flutes and bells. They were watched by three 'bemused' policemen and a couple of abusive drunks who, in the opinion of one of the chanters, sabotaged their efforts by 'frightening the spirits'.

When asked why the group wanted to levitate the station to Bermondsey, one girl told the reporter 'Because it's so ugly,' a view shared by one of the police officers who agreed that it 'Isn't a pretty building'. The girl also pointed out that Bermondsey didn't have a railway station.

St Pancras was generally seen as an eyesore in the 1960s and there was even a plan to demolish it, but the poet and Victorian Society secretary Sir John Betjeman (1906–84) got wind of it (he was tipped off by a British Rail employee) and the building was given Grade I status in 1967. Today there is a statue of Betjeman at the station.

St Pancras station.

In addition to its poor architectural reputation in the 1960s, St Pancras also tended to attract poor people. The previous year the station appeared in the opening scene of the George Melly-scripted movie *Smashing Time*. When the two northern lasses Brenda (Rita Tushingham) and Yvonne (Lynn Redgrave) arrive by train in Swinging London, they ask an Irish drunk (George A. Cooper) the way to Carnaby Street, but he leads them to Camden Street.

## Harley House
## Nos 27–50 Marylebone Road
## London, NW1 5HG

Mick Jagger lived in a flat at Harley House, an impressive Edwardian apartment building that stands on the north side of the Marylebone Road, near Regent's Park. He shared it first with Chrissie Simpson, the inspiration for the Stones song '19th Nervous Breakdown', and then with Marianne Faithfull, the inspiration for 'Let's Spend the Night Together' and 'You Can't Always Get What You Want'.

Marianne Faithfull dedicates a chapter to Harley House in her autobiography, *Faithfull*, which was published in 1994. She recounts that she moved in in 1967 and that she and Jagger later moved to Chester Square, before buying a house in Cheyne Walk.

The book also mentions Nigel (Lesmoir) Gordon, whom Marianne Faithfull calls 'one of those useful creatures one did acid with,' and his wife Jenny. They were visitors to Harley House and Nigel Lesmoir-Gordon recalled:

> Jenny and I went over there one evening, he was with Marianne, and we had some of this DMT, Diamethyl Tetrachloride, I think it's called. We dissolved the crystals into mint and smoked it. Well, this amazing substance, you smoke it and the effect lasts about 10 minutes but you go in a matter of seconds from here to infinity, you just go straight out with no messing, you just 'Brrrfff!' you go, and as we were coming down, Mick got up and he put on the turntable *Their Satanic Majesties Request* and the first track was She's Like a Rainbow.

*Their Satanic Majesties Request* was released on Friday 8 December 1967. In *Faithfull* Marianne Faithfull calls Jenny 'Jenny Ormsby-Gore'. Her real name was in fact Jenny Wallis, while Jane Ormsby-Gore was a more prominent figure in Swinging London. *She was mainly associated with*

Harley House.

*the clothes shop Hung on You and is thought to have been the inspiration for the song 'Lady Jane' on the album Aftermath, which was released on Friday 15 April 1966.*

Harley House, which is near Harley Street, was built in 1905.

# The Roundhouse
# Chalk Farm Road
# London, NW1 8EH

The Roundhouse on Chalk Farm Road was the scene of several '60s happenings. A roundhouse is a large building that contains a railway table, and this is how it started life in 1846. It only served this role for a few years, however. Advances in steam train technology soon made it redundant and in 1869 it became a warehouse for Gilbey's Gin. It fulfilled this role for the next fifty years but was then abandoned.

Things changed in 1960 when the TUC (Trade Union Congress) passed 'Resolution 42', which called for 'an enquiry into the state of the arts'. The following year Centre 42, a specific project to make the arts available to TUC members, in other words the working classes, was founded, with the playwright Arnold Wesker as its artistic director. Wesker thought this Victorian rail shed would be perfect as the organisation's main venue and, after lengthy negotiations with the owner of the lease, he was granted his wish in 1964.

Yet support for the project from Harold Wilson's Labour government was at best tepid and, as a token of his frustration, Wesker turned down a CBE in 1967. The Roundhouse therefore remained empty and members of London's growing underground scene noticed this. Record producer and UFO co-founder Joe Boyd takes up the story:

> In that year, starting from '65 to '66 to '67, one thing seemed to lead to another, and the London Free School was very idealistic and had a lot of good ideas, but it was hard to get a lot of people very excited about it as an institution, and Hoppy, John Hopkins, he, together with (Barry) Miles from Indica bookstore, which was the underground bookstore, they started the *International Times* newspaper, and they had a big party in October 1966, in the Roundhouse. And the atmosphere in the party was great: Pink Floyd and Soft Machine both played. It was a gathering of 'freaks,' I guess, you could call it – I mean, we liked the word better than 'hippie' – a lot of very creative, very strange people all in one place, and the energy was great.

Beatle Paul McCartney was a supporter of Indica and thus attended the IT party on Saturday 15 October. He dressed as an Arab Sheikh, in the company of his girlfriend Jane Asher, while Marianne Faithfull went as a nun, but in an unconventional habit that revealed most of her posterior. Michelangelo Antonioni, who was working on his film *Blow-Up*, was also a guest, as was his 'muse' and fellow Italian Monica Vitti, who that year had appeared with Terence Stamp and Dirk Bogarde in Joseph Losey's less satisfactory movie, *Modesty Blaise*.

In 2005, nearly forty years later, Pink Floyd drummer Nick Mason was asked to describe his favourite 1960s moment. He answered: 'Well, I still remember the first Roundhouse event, which was the launch of IT, because it was so shambolic. It was terrific, it was exactly how things were done. Everybody piled in, electricity was found, people set up lights. It was like "Summer Holiday on Acid". Let's do the show right here!'

The Roundhouse was to host a rather different get together the following July. (Barry) Miles recalls: 'Out of the '60s did come the environmental movement, which began to a certain extent here with the Dialectics of Liberation Conference at the Roundhouse in 1967. Gregory Bateson first gave a talk on global warming, which was the first time I'd ever heard it mentioned, and he was, of course, dismissed as a crank!'

The Dialectics of Liberation Conference was organised by the 'anti-psychiatrist' R. D. Laing. Other speakers included German Marxist philosopher Herbert Marcuse, Black Panther leader Stokely Carmichael, Michael X, Allen Ginsberg, Timothy Leary, Julian Beck of the Living Theatre and Emmett Grogan of the Diggers. In his memoir *Give the Anarchist a Cigarette*, *International Times* journalist and Deviants lead singer Mick Farren recalled that Carmichael gave a speech to an enthusiastic audience, only to announce at the end that it had been written by Adolf Hitler. The Deviants performed at the Conference and Farren recalls, with a certain pride, that this was when he received his first blow job (from a lady whose name he never learned) as a rock star. More importantly, perhaps, Farren saw the Conference's descent into argument and chaos as symptomatic of the ineffectiveness of intellectual discussion in the '60s.

Jenny Fabian includes the Roundhouse in her book *Groupie*. This was because she had worked for Middle Earth, which moved from Covent Garden to the Roundhouse in July 1968. She calls the Roundhouse 'The Big Tower'. She remembers:

> Great bands there, The Doors, Jefferson Airplane, people like that, David Bowie, five-pound group at the end of the night: just starting out, he was. I remember him coming round to my flat and asking if he could play at Middle Earth, and he got put on as the five-pound group. Well, he was a solo act, so he played on his own for five pounds at the end of the night. He was only starting out, so good for him, but it's funny to think of it!

Middle Earth's move to the Roundhouse more or less coincided with the birth of *Time Out* magazine, which produced its first listings for 12 August to 2 September. It tells us that Arthur Brown played at the Roundhouse on Saturday 17 August, and that John Mayall did so on Friday 23 August, while a 'Magical Mystery Tour (to destination unknown)' featuring Traffic, the Bonzo Dog Doo-Dah Band, Free, The Deviants, Fairport Convention and the Incredible String Band, was billed for Saturday 24 August and Sunday 25th. The Doors and Jefferson Airplane, on the other hand, played on a double bill on Friday 6 September and Saturday 7th.

The Roundhouse finally became a fully fledged arts venue in 1969 and continued as such until it closed, through lack of funding, in 1983 (Wesker having resigned in 1972). It reopened in 1996 and was refurbished between 2004 and 2006.

The Roundhouse.

# NW8

## Abbey Road
## No. 3 Abbey Road
## London, NW8 9AY

Abbey Road received the ultimate accolade of providing the title of a Beatles album (which was released in the UK on Friday 26 September 1969, and in the United States on Wednesday 1 October). If you make the trek to Abbey Road, the recording studios are relatively easy to find; simply look for the fans of all ages who have come from around the world to scrawl graffiti on the walls and get their photographs taken on the famous zebra crossing (which, like the studios, enjoys Grade II listed status).

And yet, until the Beatles came along, the famous recording studio was rarely referred to as 'Abbey Road' – its official name was 'EMI Studios'. In his 1968 book, *The Beatles*, for example, Hunter Davies states that the Fab Four first auditioned for George Martin at 'EMI's Number Three Studio in St John's Wood' on Thursday 6 June 1962. EMI didn't adopt the Abbey Road name until 1970.

The recording studios were – and still are – housed in an 1830s building, which had originally functioned as a large family home. The Gramophone Company (later Electric and Musical Industries) bought it in 1931 and turned it into three (and then four) studios. Sir Edward Edgar (conducting Land of Hope of Glory, in Studio One that year), Sir Malcolm Sargent and Cliff Richard all made recordings there prior to George Martin and the Beatles.

The Beatles recorded most of their work at Abbey Road and Jill Furmanovsky, who was a teenager in the 1960s, recalls:

Yes, I used to stand outside Abbey Road studios with lots of other Beatle fans. I used to go there after school, or in school holidays, and the Beatles used to come; they each had a Mini with darkened windows, and they'd roll up in the Minis and, if they were in a good mood, they might sign an autograph, or say hello to the fans. And Paul McCartney lived just up the road in Cavendish Avenue, so sometimes we'd wait there and I once took a picture of him outside his house with my schoolfriends, on an instamatic. I also remember Mal Evans, who was their tour manager, he used to send us girls on errands; we used to have to go buy some milk for their tea, and stuff like that, and we were always thrilled if he came out and so on.

In the 1970s Jill Furmanovsky would become the concert photographer for Pink Floyd (and she would later use this work and that of other rock photographers when she founded the organisation rockarchive.com). Pink Floyd first went to Abbey Road in February 1967 to start work on their first album, *A Piper at the Gates of Dawn*. This was the same month that the Beatles were putting the finishing touches to 'A Day in the Life', the last track on *Sgt. Pepper*.

And on Sunday 25 June that year something else happened. (Barry) Miles explains:

And I was there, for instance, at the 'All You Need is Love' session, which was the first time Telstar [Intelsat – ed.], or whatever it was, had been used to connect up TV stations all around the world, and most countries had an example of sort of clog dancing or something, but the Beatles, of course, were chosen to represent Britain, and so this was like the great high moment of British rock 'n' roll culture. And John Lennon mostly wrote the song which, since he recognised that the vast majority of people watching it on TV wouldn't be English speakers, he kept it really, really simple, just 'All You Need is Love' and that's pretty much the only lyrics that the thing's got!

The programme, which was called *Our World*, included Maria Callas and Pablo Picasso. The broadcast was watched by an estimated 400 million viewers in twenty-six countries. Miles adds:

And it turned into an enormous party held at Abbey Road studios, the big studio there, and everyone was all dressed up in their finest psychedelic clothing. There were balloons and there were joints and there were great big bunches of incense burning, it was like an incredible party. And the idea was, obviously, very naively, to spread the message that 'All You Need Is Love' you know, right across the world, and beam out good vibes from London. And looking back, I mean, like I say, it was a bit naive, but at the time it was fantastic, I mean, there was a tremendous feeling there, really positive: good vibes in fact, that's what it was!

Even though this was only a few days before their appearances at Chichester Court (following the Redlands bust in February), Mick Jagger and Keith Richards were present at Abbey Road's Studio One, as were Marianne Faithfull, Jane Asher and Keith Moon. 'All You Need Is Love' closed the *Our World* broadcast. The song was released as a single in the UK on Friday 7 July and went straight to number one.

Abbey Road.

# No. 7 Cavendish Avenue
# London, NW8 9JG

This large house has been the home of Paul (now Sir Paul) McCartney since 1966. Paul was the only Beatle who decided to continue living in London: John, George and Ringo and their partners all moved out to homes in Surrey's 'Stockbroker Belt'. McCartney chose the property for its proximity to Abbey Road, and it was here that much of the writing and rehearsal for the group's later albums took place. Other Beatle business was discussed here: Peter Blake came round to present the cover for *Sgt. Pepper*, while the EMI chairman, Sir Joseph Lockwood, once paid a visit in his Rolls-Royce, in order to settle a contractual issue.

According to Hunter Davies (in his book *The Beatles*), McCartney bought the house in late 1966, but according to *The Beatles London*, he acquired it in March 1965 and moved in in August 1966. It is agreed that the price was £40,000 (a fortune at that time) and that the previous owner was a doctor, one Desmond O'Neill. Prior to that, Paul had been a lodger at the family home of his actress girlfriend, Jane Asher, at No. 57 Wimpole Street.

Paul and Jane were still very much an item during the first two years at Cavendish Avenue. Hunter Davies was given access for his book, *The Beatles*, and he describes the domestic setting. The other resident was, of course, Martha, the large, lovable Old English sheepdog immortalised in the song 'Martha My Dear'. Davies observes that 'Paul and Jane are a very loving couple,' while we also learn that 'When Jane is not working, she does a lot of the cooking, and she is very good.' Davies' book was published in 1968, prior to Paul and Jane's break-up. This allegedly happened after she discovered Paul with another woman at Cavendish Avenue.

Barry Fantoni was also a visitor to the house. This was after he had helped Paul buy a harmonium from an old friend from his Camberwell Art School days, Paddy Lovely. Not only that, he had then driven Paul and the harmonium back to Cavendish Avenue. He recalls:

And we got the Harmonium back and I helped him put into his front room – well, it wasn't a front room, it was the kind of the foyer of this vast freestanding house which had its own gaslight outside and Jane Asher inside. And we put the harmonium on the deck and he sat down and played the riff that John Lennon wrote for 'We Can Work it Out', and said, 'Oh, it's a great sound this.' I then went home, but in the morning, unusually early, the phone rang and he said, 'Oh, man, it's Paul. Have you got some time to come over and that? Because I've written this song and want your opinion on it and that.' So I went over and he had written 'Your Mother Should Know', and he was very pleased with it and he sang 'We Can Work It Out' as well. And I was very struck at the time by the lyrics because they were actually prescient. At this time he was shagging another bird and Jane got to find out about it and, actually, they didn't work it out! Well, they did: they got separated and she ended up by marrying Gerald Scarfe, who was the caricaturist on *Private Eye* and *The Sunday Times*, and she later found her true vocation, which was never acting but baking cakes and decorating them in vile colours, a bit like Gerry's drawings, really! (see 22 Cale Street, page 83]

Cavendish Avenue had a garden wall, gate and intercom system, designed to keep the many Beatles fans at bay, although Paul would often appear and sign autographs. It is said that a desperate Brian Epstein rang the intercom a few days before his death, but that Paul, thinking it was just another fan, didn't answer. Brian then had to call Paul from a pay phone at St John's Wood Underground station.

Nearby, at No. 1 Cavendish Avenue, there is a 'Musical Heritage' plaque indicating the former home of another Liverpudlian singer: Billy Fury, who died in 1983. The Silver Beetles had an audition in Liverpool on Wednesday 10 May 1960 in order to become his backing group, but they were turned down by Larry Parnes.

No. 7 Cavendish Avenue.

# N8

## Hornsey College of Art
## No. 77 Crouch End Hill
## London, N8 8DN

Ray Davies of the Kinks was a student at Hornsey College of Art in the early 1960s, as was Deep Purple bassist Roger Glover, but on Tuesday 28 May 1968 this institution attracted attention for a different reason. Its students began what has variously been termed a 24-hour 'work-in', 'teach-in' and 'sleep-in', but as David Page, a teacher at the college, recalled in an account that he wrote for The Tate, 'it turned into a six-week occupation'.

Student protest had been brewing at Hornsey College of Art for some time. As was the case elsewhere, part of it was against the Vietnam War. Nick Wright, a student leader who would later be expelled from the college, relates in a separate account that the previous year '£100 (four times a policeman's wage in 1967) was collected from students by the Young Communist League to buy a motorbike for the Viet Cong'. The situation at Hornsey heated up after the events in Paris in early May 1968, but there were other, local factors. The grievances of the students and the members of staff who supported them included dissatisfaction with the curriculum and concern for the 'Polytechnic Plan'. This was a scheme to incorporate Hornsey along with Enfield Technical College and Hendon Technical Institute into a new polytechnic. The building at Crouch End Hill wasn't in fact the only Hornsey campus: there were others at what Wright calls 'a scruffy civil defence building on the North Circular Road,' while sculpture students were taught at the Alexandra Palace. According to David Page, the protesting students had a utopian vision for their college: 'What we aimed to do was simple: as William Blake put it, to build Jerusalem.'

The students took over the campus and even ran it, but they were forcibly removed six weeks later. Wright says that this was at the instigation of the local (Conservative-run) council: 'Barbed wire and Alsatians enforced a six-month lock-out.' Page refers to this as 'The Day of the Dogs,' when a team of security men with Alsatians were sent to surround and seal off the main building,' adding that 'students tamed the dogs with biscuits, and the whole episode collapsed into a farce'.

Questions were asked in Parliament about the heavy-handed tactics of the security men, but Shirley Williams, the Minister of State for Education and Science in Harold Wilson's Labour government, appeared to wash her hands of the matter, telling the House of Commons: 'We have been in touch with the local authority. We have no power over the decisions which the local authorities make concerning the day-today running of their colleges. While we deplore the use of force wherever it can be avoided, this is a matter which lies directly and wholly within the responsibility of the Hornsey local authority.'

Hornsey College of Art.

The protesters may have been bloodied, but they were unbowed. In April 1969 they staged a mock funeral procession (the 'Hornsey Weep In') for the 'death of Hornsey Hope' and delivered a petition to No. 10 Downing Street.

Nevertheless, the Polytechnic Plan went ahead. Middlesex Polytechnic was founded in 1973 and Nick Wright was reinstated and allowed to complete his degree there in the 1980s. The polytechnic became Middlesex University in 1992. As for the Crouch End campus, it later became the TUC Education Centre, and today it is the home of Coleridge Primary School.

# N22

## Alexandra Palace
## Alexandra Palace Way
## London, N22 7AY

The Alexandra Palace (also known as 'the Ally Pally' and even 'the People's Palace') was an important musical venue throughout the 1960s. As George Melly recounted in his 1970 book *Revolt into Style*, it hosted an 'all-night rave' in 1961, while the Rolling Stones played at another all-night rave there on Saturday 6 June 1964. Yet the most famous event was undoubtedly the 14-Hour Technicolor Dream on Saturday 29 April 1967.

The purpose of the exercise was ostensibly to raise funds for the *International Times*, which was still smarting from the police raid of Monday 9 March. The line-up included Soft Machine, the Crazy World of Arthur Brown, the Pretty Things, Move, Creation, the Purple Gang, Alex Harvey and, last but not least, Pink Floyd, who virtually crowned themselves kings of the underground that night, even if Syd Barrett was by now in a bad way. Indeed, the event was so big that John Lennon and John Dunbar turned up to take a look, although they don't seem to have taken much interest in *Cut Piece*, Yoko Ono's bra-cutting 'happening'.

It all sounds to have been wonderful, but it wasn't to everybody's liking. *Groupie* author Jenny Fabian confessed, for example, that 'I didn't really enjoy it, actually. It was too big, that one. I like to be, in a way, cocooned into the music, and they had three or bands all playing at once that night. I couldn't sort of settle, and I felt out of my ground, as it were, I felt unfamiliar up there. And I listened and I saw the Floyd and I thought they were fantastic, but I was quite glad when it was all over'.

Jonathon Green, who was then an undergraduate at Oxford, also thinks that it was probably less 'way out' than we tend to imagine. He says, 'If you look at a picture of the Ally Pally that night, and you look at the haircuts, you will see that most of them are short, that the predominant garment is probably the duffle coat, and so on and so forth.'

Yet Deviants lead singer and *IT* journalist Mick Farren had a great time:

> I don't actually know what the Alexandra Palace looks like inside in daylight, but I mean this vast area with the huge pipe organ at one end, and there were bands playing at both ends of the hall simultaneously. And I was standing quite close to John Lennon in the sort of mixing spot in the middle where both bands blurred into each other, and he's leaning this way and leaning that way and kind of grinning and I was doing the same thing, then we clopped each other.

Alexandra Palace.

Mick Farren also liked the setting: 'It was a gorgeous place. If you wandered out there were fountains, old broken-down fountains, it was kind of like some kind of gutted, gorgeous old palace after a revolution or something.'

Roger Bunn, who was a member of the group Giant Sun Trolley, also enjoyed himself: 'And it was huge and everybody was totally spaced and the next day it didn't actually stop. When the music stopped, it didn't actually stop because right outside there's all greenery and gardens and things, so the next day everybody was recovering in these gardens, all totally spaced out, and out of it on all the great music they'd heard at the time.'

The 14-Hour Technicolor Dream was a roaring success, even if, as Mick Farren admitted in his book *Give the Anarchist a Cigarette*, nobody really knows what happened to the money it raised. A few months later, on Saturday 29 July, the 'Ally Pally' hosted another event: The Love-In International Festival, which featured performances by, among others, Pink Floyd, the Crazy World of Arthur Brown, Brian Auger, Julie Driscoll and Trinity, and Eric Burdon and the Animals.

Alexandra Palace was built in 1873 as North London's answer to the Crystal Palace, which had been dismantled and moved to South London from Hyde Park after the Great Exhibition of 1851. In 1936 (the year that Crystal Palace was destroyed by fire) Alexandra Palace was used for the world's first television broadcast. Alexandra Palace had its own fire in 1980, but it was restored and reopened in 1988.

# Bibliography

Beatles, The *The Beatles Anthology* (Weidenfeld & Nicolson, 2001)

Boyd, Joe, *White Bicycles Making Music in the 1960s* (Serpent's Tail, 2006)

Dallas, Karl; Barry Fantoni, *Swinging London: A Guide to Where the Action Is* (Stanmore Press Limited, 1967)

Davenport-Hines, Richard, *An English Affair: Sex, Class and Power in the Age of Profumo* (Harper Press, 2013)

Davies, Hunter, *The Beatles* (Ebury Press, 2009)

Davies, Hunter, *The New London Spy* (Anthony Blond, 1966)

Deighton, Len, *The Ipcress File* (Harper, 2009)

Deighton, Len, *Len Deighton's London Dossier* (Penguin Books, 1967)

DiLello, Richard, *The Longest Cocktail Party: An Insider's Diary of The Beatles, Their Million-dollar Apple Empire and its Wild Rise & Fall* (Canongate, 2005)

Diski, Jenny, *The Sixties* (Profile Books, 2009)

Fabian Jenny; Johnny Byrne, *Groupie* (Omnibus Press, 1997)

Faithfull, Marianne with David Dalton, *Faithfull* (Penguin Books, 1995)

Fantoni, Barry, *A Whole Scene Going On My Inside Story of Private Eye, the Pop Revolution and Swinging Sixties London* (Polygon, 2019)

Farren, Mick, *Give the Anarchist a Cigarette* (Pimlico, 2002)

*Gear Guide 1967* (Old House, 2013)

Green, Jonathon, *Days in the Life: Voices from the English Underground 1961–1971* (Minerva, 1989)

Green, Jonathon, *All Dressed Up: The Sixties and Counterculture* (Pimlico 1990)

Gross Alex, *The Untold 60s* (Cross-Cultural Research Projects, 2010)

Halasz, Piri, *A Swinger's Guide to London* (iUniverse, Bloomington, 2010)

Hathaway, Norman, Dan Nadel, *Electrical Banana: Masters of Psychedelic Art* (Damiano, 2011)

Hulanicki, Barbara, *From A to Biba: The Autobiography of Barbara Hulanicki* (V&A Publishing, 2018)

Levin, Bernard, *The Pendulum Years Britain and the Sixties* (Pan Books, 1972)

Levy, Shawn, *Ready, Steady, Go! Swinging London and the Invention of Cool* (Fourth Estate, 2003)

Melly, George, *Revolt into Style: The Pop Arts in Britain* (Penguin Books, 1972)

Metzger, Rainer, *London in the Sixties* (Thames & Hudson, 2012)

Miles, Barry, *In the Sixties* (Pimlico 2003)

Miles, Barry, *Hippie* (Cassell Illustrated, 2003)

Miles, Barry, *London Calling: A Countercultural History of London Since 1945* (Atlantic Books, 2010)

Nairn, Ian, *Nairn's London* (Penguin Books, 2014)

Neville, Richard, *Playpower* (Paladin, 1971)

Nuttall, Jeff, *Bomb Culture* (Paladin, 1970)

Overbury, Steve, *The Beatles and the Stones in the Swinging Sixties* (Stephen Overbury, 2009)

Richards, Keith, *Life* (Phoenix, 2011)

Richler, Mordechai, *Cocksure* (Vintage, 1992)

Schreuders, Piet, Mark Lewisohn and Adam Smith, *The Beatles' London* (Portico, 2008)

Sutherland, Alasdair Scott, *The Spaghetti Tree Mario and Franco and the Trattoria Revolution* (Primavera, 2009)

Vyner, Harriet, *Groovy Bob: The Life and Times of Robert Fraser* (Faber and Faber, 1999)

Walker, Alexander, *Hollywood England: The British Film Industry in the Sixties* (Orion Books, 2005)

Wheen, Francis, *The Sixties* (Ebury Press, 1982)